The Sovereignty of God in Our Daily Lives

To and for the Glory of God!

Man's Salvation is for God, of God, by God, in God,
through God, because of God, for the Glory of God,
lest any man would boast

David R. Rosen

ISBN 978-1-63874-188-6 (paperback)
ISBN 978-1-63874-189-3 (digital)

Christian Faith Publishing, Inc.
832 Park Avenue
Meadville, PA 16335
www.christianfaithpublishing.com

Scripture quotations are from the ESV® Bible (The Holy Bible, English Standard Version®), copyright © 2001 by Crossway, a publishing ministry of Good News Publishers. Used by permission. All rights reserved.

Printed in the United States of America

The Sovereignty of God in Our Daily Lives

The heart of man plans his way, but the Lord establishes his steps.
—Proverbs 16:9

Then the Lord said to me, "You have seen well, for
I am watching over my word to perform it."
—Jeremiah 1:12

The Lord of hosts has sworn: "As I have planned, so shall
it be, and as I have purposed, so shall it stand."
—Isaiah 14:24

I will say to the north, Give up, and to the south, Do not
withhold; bring my sons from afar and my daughters from
the end of the earth, everyone who is called by my name,
whom I created for my glory, whom I formed and made.
—Isaiah 43:6–7

For it is God who works in you to will and to
act in order to fulfill his good purpose.
—Philippians 2:13

For by grace you have been saved through faith. And
this is not your own doing; it is the gift of God, not a
result of works, so that no one may boast. For we are his
workmanship, created in Christ Jesus for good works, which
God prepared beforehand, that we should walk in them.
—Ephesians 2:8–10

That the God of our Lord Jesus Christ, the Father of glory,
may give you the Spirit of wisdom and of revelation in the
knowledge of him, having the eyes of your hearts enlightened,
that you may know what is the hope to which he has called
you, what are the riches of his glorious inheritance in the saints,
and what is the immeasurable greatness of his power toward
us who believe, according to the working of his great might.

—Ephesians 1:17–19

So, whether you eat or drink, or whatever
you do, do all to the glory of God.

—1 Corinthians 10:31

Contents

Father, I praise You for who You are, for Your will to be done, and for the glory You deserve, for Your name is above all names and is to be highly exalted! May You be glorified in our studies and that You would open our hearts to the truth of Your word. In Jesus's name I ask, amen.

Preface

To God the Father

To the glory and perfect will of God the Father, who, before creation, willed all things to be. Who always was and who is and who will always be. From man's limited comprehension of the glory of God the Father, who is the father of our Lord Jesus Christ, He is the Great I AM, who, at a point in time, (who, by the way, also created and establishes time) revealed a veiled part of His glory to Moses. Who spoke to Moses (Exod. 6:2; Mark 12:26) as well as to Abraham (Gen. 22:1–2), and to Peter, James, and John (Matt. 17:5). And now through His Son, by His Spirit through His word, reveals to us His salvation in and through Jesus Christ. (For no man comes to the Father except through Jesus Christ.)

And in all things, it pleased God the Father to have His Son Jesus be the visual "doer" of His will—in and always according to the counsel of the Father's will. And further, it pleased the Father for Jesus to die for man's sin—in accordance with obedience to the will of God the Father. And as love toward Jesus, and in plan before the world began, God the Father also purposed Jesus's sheep as objects of His love for the Son. For God the Father not only had in view and plan of His Son dying for the sins of all who would believe in Him but also each one He has purposed to be in Christ and His Spirit in them.

> All that the Father gives me will come to me, and
> whoever comes to me I will never cast out. For I

have come down from heaven, not to do my own will but the will of him who sent me. And this is the will of him who sent me, that I should lose nothing of all that he has given me, but raise it up on the last day. For this is the will of my Father, that everyone who looks on the Son and believes in him should have eternal life, and I will raise him up on the last day. (John 6:37–39)

To God the Son—Jesus Christ

Who is the creator of all things; who is in the center of all things; and in all things, He holds, He sustains, and He keeps; to the glory of God the Father. For…

In the beginning was the Word, and the Word was with God, and the Word was God. He was in the beginning with God. All things were made through him, and without him was not any thing made that was made. (John 1:1–3)

He [Jesus] is the image of the invisible God, the firstborn of all creation. For by Him all things were created, both in the heavens and on earth, visible and invisible, whether thrones or dominions or rulers or authorities—all things have been created through Him and for Him. He is before all things, and in Him all things hold together. He is also head of the body, the church; and He is the beginning, the firstborn from the dead, so that He Himself will come to have first place in everything. For it was the Father's good pleasure for all the fullness to dwell in Him, and through Him to reconcile all things to Himself, having made peace through the blood of His cross; through Him, I say, whether things on earth or things in heaven. And although you were formerly alienated and hostile in mind, engaged in evil deeds, yet He has now reconciled you in His fleshly body through death, in order to present you before Him holy and blameless and beyond reproach—if indeed you continue in the faith firmly established and steadfast, and not moved away from the hope of the gospel that you have heard, which was proclaimed in all creation under heaven, and of which I, Paul, was made a minister. (Col. 1:15–23)

To God the Spirit, the Giver of Life

To the physical

The Spirit of God has made me, and the breath of the Almighty gives me life. (Job 33:4)

To the spiritual

It is the Spirit who gives life; the flesh is no help at all. The words that I have spoken to you are spirit and life. (John 6:63)

For the law of the Spirit of life has set you free in Christ Jesus from the law of sin and death. For God has done what the law, weakened by the flesh, could not do. By sending his own Son in the likeness of sinful flesh and for sin, he condemned sin in the flesh, in order that the righteous requirement of the law might be fulfilled in us, who walk not according to the flesh but according to the Spirit. For those who live according to the flesh set their minds on the things of the flesh, but those who live according to the

Spirit set their minds on the things of the Spirit. For to set the mind on the flesh is death, but to set the mind on the Spirit is life and peace. For the mind that is set on the flesh is hostile to God, for it does not submit to God's law; indeed, it cannot. Those who are in the flesh cannot please God. You, however, are not in the flesh but in the Spirit, if in fact the Spirit of God dwells in you. Anyone who does not have the Spirit of Christ does not belong to him. But if Christ is in you, although the body is dead because of sin, the Spirit is life because of righteousness. If the Spirit of him who raised Jesus from the dead dwells in you, he who raised Christ Jesus from the dead will also give life to your mortal bodies through his Spirit who dwells in you. (Rom. 8:2–11)

Who is our comforter and witness of truth

So the church throughout all Judea and Galilee and Samaria had peace and was being built up. And walking in the fear of the Lord and in the comfort of the Holy Spirit, it multiplied. (Acts 9:31)

But when the Helper comes, whom I will send to you from the Father, the Spirit of truth, who proceeds from the Father, he will bear witness about me. And you also will bear witness, because you have been with me from the beginning. (John 15:26–27)

Who facilitates God's love into our hearts

And hope does not put us to shame, because God's love has been poured into our hearts through the Holy Spirit who has been given to us. (Rom. 5:5)

And He is our wisdom

These things God has revealed to us through the Spirit. For the Spirit searches everything, even the depths of God. For who knows a person's thoughts except the spirit of that person, which is in him? So also no one comprehends the thoughts of God except the Spirit of God. Now we have received not the spirit of the world, but the Spirit who is from God, that we might understand the things freely given us by God. And we impart this in words not taught by human wisdom but taught by the Spirit, interpreting spiritual truths to those who are spiritual. The natural person does not accept the things of the Spirit of God, for they are folly to him, and he is not able to understand them because they are spiritually discerned. The spiritual person judges all things, but is himself to be judged by no one. "For who has understood the mind of the Lord so as to instruct him?" But we have the mind of Christ. (1 Cor. 2:10–17)

For this reason, because I have heard of your faith in the Lord Jesus and your love toward all the saints, I do not cease to give thanks for you, remembering you in my prayers, that the God of our Lord Jesus Christ, the Father of glory, may give you the Spirit of wisdom and of revelation in the knowledge of him, having the eyes of your hearts enlightened, that you may know what is the hope to which he has called you, what are the riches of his glorious inheritance in the saints, and

> what is the immeasurable greatness of his power
> toward us who believe, according to the working
> of his great might that he worked in Christ when
> he raised him from the dead and seated him at
> his right hand in the heavenly places, far above all
> rule and authority and power and dominion, and
> above every name that is named, not only in this
> age but also in the one to come. (Eph. 1:15–21)

God the Father, God the Son, God the Spirit—they are persons, as best as man can comprehend. And yet there is but one God.

> Jesus answered, "The most important is, 'Hear,
> O Israel: The Lord our God, the Lord is one. And
> you shall love the Lord your God with all your
> heart and with all your soul and with all your
> mind and with all your strength.' The second is
> this: 'You shall love your neighbor as yourself.'
> There is no other commandment greater than
> these." (Mark 12:29–31)

Disciples, Apostles, and Pharisees

For the aim again of this book is to guide you in your biblical studies in seeing God's working in your life, in the steps He has purposed specifically for you before the world began. So that in knowing it is all God's work—of His calling, of His revealing, in His enabling, of His saving, and of His sanctifying you, to the wisdom given to you of His Son Jesus Christ by His Spirit working within you and through you—to the good works He has prepared for you to walk in. In your working, in your walking—by His holding, in His keeping—individually to you, as part of the people He has sanctified for Himself from before His creation—belonging now to Jesus Christ, who are known by His name, that is—in His revelation to you AND, with His wisdom in enablement for you—to see and understand, to live in obedience, and to rest in His assurance—that your joy now known deeper in Christ would be made full. That by His Spirit, as His word is read, you could now have a fuller understanding of the wonder of the salvation you have been called to—with His wisdom and knowledge of how precious and special Jesus is to you.

The apostles, they daily walked with Jesus while Jesus was alive in teaching and preaching the Gospel of salvation, and yet they did not fully comprehend the fullness of who Jesus was until He opened their mind to the scriptures.

> And beginning with Moses and all the Prophets, he interpreted to them in all the Scriptures the things concerning himself. Then he said to them, "These are my words that I spoke to you while I was still with you, that everything written about me in the Law of Moses and the Prophets and the Psalms must be fulfilled." Then he opened their minds to understand the Scriptures. (Luke 24:27, 44–45)

Conversely, the Pharisees, Scribes, and Sadducees of the day, the ones who were supposed to know the scriptures and understand what they meant, did not know (or maybe better stated, did not want to believe) that Jesus was their Messiah standing before them, for they wallowed in their own stature in society and of their self-religiosity, for they despised what Jesus was doing to upset their religious position by always trying to trap Jesus, for which Jesus always pointed back to their ignorance of the scriptures:

> He said to them, "Have you not read what David did when he was hungry, and those who were with him: how he entered the house of God and ate the bread of the Presence, which it was not lawful for him to eat nor for those who were with him, but only for the priests? Or have you not read in the Law how on the Sabbath the priests in the temple profane the Sabbath and are guiltless?

I tell you, something greater than the temple is here. And <u>if you had known what this means</u>, 'I desire mercy, and not sacrifice,' you would not have condemned the guiltless. For the Son of Man is lord of the Sabbath." (Matt. 12:3–8)

Without God's Enablement, Scriptures Are Just Words

As the Pharisees used scripture to add to their stature and wealth, they lacked need—humility—for they received what they saw and not what Scripture showed.

For since, in the wisdom of God, the world did not know God through wisdom, it pleased God through the folly of what we preach to save those who believe. For Jews demand signs and Greeks seek wisdom, but we preach Christ crucified, a stumbling block to Jews and folly to Gentiles, but to those who are called, both Jews and Greeks, Christ the power of God and the wisdom of God. (1 Cor. 1:21–24)

For consider your calling, brothers: not many of you were wise according to worldly standards, not many were powerful, not many were of noble birth. But God chose what is foolish in the world to shame the wise; God chose what is weak in the world to shame the strong; God chose what is low and despised in the world, even things that are not, to bring to nothing things that are, so that no human being might boast in the presence of God. And because of him you are in Christ Jesus, who became to us wisdom from God, righteousness and sanctification and redemption, so that, as it is written, "Let the one who boasts, boast in the Lord." (1 Cor. 1:26–31)

> For by grace you have been saved through faith. And this is not your own doing; it is the gift of God, not a result of works, so that no one may boast. For we are his workmanship, created in Christ Jesus for good works, which God prepared beforehand, that we should walk in them. (Eph. 2:8–10)

The Wisdom of God, the Wisdom from God

His Spirit opening our minds to the truth of the Gospel is God's workings in us and not we ourselves.

Going back to John 6, to when the huge crowds were following Jesus, and Jesus calls them out for why they are following, for provision and food and not for repentance and Jesus's righteousness, Jesus takes the step of separation to say to the crowd,

> It is written in the Prophets, "And they will all be taught by God." Everyone who has heard and learned from the Father comes to me. [Does not this look familiar with Ezekiel 31:31–34?] (John 6:45)

And then He speaks to them spiritually by saying that He is the bread of life and that they need to eat of His flesh and drink of His blood and not to the food they were given, not even to the manna that Moses gave them. And even to that, Jesus says Moses did not feed them the true food of heaven, for it was the Father who gave them the true bread from heaven that is Jesus.

> Then they said to him, "What must we do, to be doing the works of God?" Jesus answered them,

21

"This is the work of God, that you believe in him
whom he has sent." (John 6:28–29)

"And they will be taught by God," for "this is the Work of God,
that you believe in Him whom He has sent." The separation of His
followers has begun.

So how did His followers respond?

When many of his disciples heard it, they said, "This is a hard
saying; who can listen to it?" But Jesus, knowing in himself that his
disciples were grumbling about this, said to them, "Do you take
offense at this? Then what if you were to see the Son of Man ascend-
ing to where he was before? It is the Spirit who gives life; **the flesh
is no help at all**. The words that I have spoken to you are spirit and
life. But there are some of you who do not believe." (For Jesus knew
from the beginning who those were who did not believe, and who
it was who would betray him.) And he said, "This is why I told you
that no one can come to me unless it is granted him by the Father."
(John 6:60–65)

Take a second to rewind. Here we see that Jesus just presented
this crowd, His disciples/followers, the Gospel. They hear the Gospel
and asked an exceptionally good question: "What must we do, to be
doing the works of God?" Jesus answered them, "This is the work of
God, that you believe in him whom he has sent."

And what was their reply? "This is a hard saying. Who can listen to it?"

Could they have responded differently? They could have. Yet
they could not have. Like the Pharisees in self-interest, they sought
after Jesus for fish and bread as Jesus had just fed the five thousand,
but not for seeking the Bread of Life, for who Jesus just told them
that He is.

They heard the Gospel directly from Jesus. They asked what
they must do. Jesus tells them directly to believe. They chose not to,
but really, they could not. For Jesus also tells them:

> Jesus answered them, "This is the work of God, that you believe in him whom he has sent." (John 6:29)

> It is written in the Prophets, "And they will all be taught by God." Everyone who has heard and learned from the Father comes to me. (John 6:45)

Now here is the view to those for whom God was working in.

> When many of his disciples heard it, they said, "This is a hard saying; who can listen to it?" But Jesus, knowing in himself that his disciples were grumbling about this, said to them, "Do you take offense at this? Then what if you were to see the Son of Man ascending to where he was before? It is the Spirit who gives life; the flesh is no help at all. The words that I have spoken to you are spirit and life. But there are some of you who do not believe." (For Jesus knew from the beginning who those were who did not believe, and who it was who would betray him.) And he said, "This is why I told you that no one can come to me unless it is granted him by the Father." After this many of his disciples turned back and no longer walked with him. So, Jesus said to the twelve, "Do you want to go away as well?" Simon Peter answered him, "Lord, to whom shall we go? You have the words of eternal life, and we have believed, and have come to know, that you are the Holy One of God." Jesus answered them, "Did I not choose you, the twelve? And yet one of you is a devil." He spoke of Judas the son of Simon Iscariot, for he, one of the twelve, was going to betray him. (John 6:60–71)

So as John writes in 1 John 5:6–12, 20, the spirit testifies with Jesus—who is the water and the blood…

> This is he who came by water and blood—Jesus Christ; not by the water only but by the water and the blood. And the Spirit is the one who testifies, because the Spirit is the truth. For there are three that testify: the Spirit and the water and the blood; and these three agree. If we receive the testimony of men, the testimony of God is greater, for this is the testimony of God that he has borne concerning his Son. Whoever believes in the Son of God has the testimony in himself. Whoever does not believe God has made him a liar, because he has not believed in the testimony that God has borne concerning his Son. And this is the testimony, that God gave us eternal life, and this life is in his Son. Whoever has the Son has life; whoever does not have the Son of God does not have life.

And we know that the Son of God has come and has given us understanding, so that we may know him who is true; and we are in him who is true, in his Son Jesus Christ. He is the true God and eternal life.

For Salvation Is of the Lord

Salvation is not for those who are self-wise in choice, nor by the good works of man to earn, but of the purposes of God. And God does not choose between one over another, nor does He relent based on external influences from Himself, but every step of His will, even the history of the world's past up to a second ago—to the very next second of the future—is accomplished as He has purposed before creation. Nor does God change His mind—or need to have a plan B as man so often does.

God is sovereign, and His will is secure. He is consistent, constant, holy, and set apart from all that He created. God created man in His image, and the earth is His footstool. He rules and reigns, and His name is above all names, and there is no other like Him. He defines the day from the night; the distant past from the future; the boundaries and actions of nations, in the rule of the land; the fullness of His goodness from the darkness of sin…for in all of His creation, he has defined, set, planned, sustained, and will accomplish in all creation—all things, and again He purposes good and evil to exist, for He himself is good, and holy, and perfect and without blemish, leading back to the opening statements that all things created are for Him, through Him, by Him, and in Him and because of Him—to the counsel of His will to the glory of His name!

His love is pure as is His wrath. He defines the bounds of His creation, and yet He himself is not confined to those bounds. He defines gravity, and yet He walked on water and ascended into the clouds. He defines the winds and the storms (Ps. 29; Matt. 8:27; Luke 8:25), and by His words, they obey His commands. And to God, the night and the day are the same to Him. Let this set in for a second. God sees day and night the same. Time does not constrain Him nor change Him. So emphasizing for understanding, all things…all things are created by Him and for Him, and all things exist, both physical and spiritual. All things are for His glory to be displayed! He is pure, He is holy, He is righteous, and He is worthy!

God's Perspective—A Treasure to Hold

Even the darkness is not dark to you; the night
is bright as the day, for darkness is as light with
you. (Ps. 139:12)

In looking at our approach to reading God's word, look at what David says about night and day from God's perspective.

"[That] darkness is not dark to God, for it is bright as the day." Day and night are the same to God.

It is with this insight we may need to challenge our own vantage point to seek to see His word within the Bible from God's higher perspective—as His Spirit guides us.

To the purpose of creation and salvation and eternity, the apostle John tells us that Jesus has a book that was written before the world was created AND that it was God's purpose that Jesus be slain for those peoples written within the Book of Life:

> All who dwell on the earth will worship him [the Antichrist], everyone whose name has not been written from the foundation of the world in the book of life of the Lamb who has been slain. (Rev. 13:8)

> Yet it was the will of the Lord to crush him; he has put him to grief; when his soul makes an offering for guilt, he shall see his offspring; he shall prolong his days; the will of the Lord shall prosper in his hand. (Isa. 53:10)

So…to the call of self-examination, that the Bible is also clear to declare. For having eyes to see and ears to hear is evidence of God's workings within you. Paul writes within Romans as a first stopping point:

> For all who are being led by the Spirit of God, these are sons of God. For you have not received a spirit of slavery leading to fear again, but you have received a spirit of adoption as sons by which we cry out, "Abba! Father!" The Spirit Himself testifies with our spirit that we are children of God, and if children, heirs also, heirs of God and fellow heirs with Christ, if indeed we suffer with Him so that we may also be glorified with Him. For I consider that the sufferings of this present time are not worthy to be compared

with the glory that is to be revealed to us. For the anxious longing of the creation waits eagerly for the revealing of the sons of God. (Rom. 8:14–19)

The Purpose of This Study

Our journey within this book is to gaze upon Christ. In love, with adoration and with praise, blessing Him for who He is, for us to see and seek His glory through His tender words writing to the history, present and future of His eternal reign and glory. The words I type mean nothing outside of being an usher to God's workings of the Gospel within you and me. For it is God who brings us both wisdom. It is God who also gives understanding, and it is God who uses man to accomplish His will, for it is God who receives the glory. For as Paul writes:

> But by the grace of God I am what I am, and his grace to me was not without effect. No, I worked harder than all of them—yet not I, but the grace of God that was with [in] me. (1 Cor. 15:10)

My Purpose in Writing

Outside of writing to glorify God, I feel within my heart to leave my children and my grandchildren and, if it should be by the grace of the Lord, their kids and their kids a reference and a legacy of Jesus Christ written by me to encourage and share the Gospel of my Lord and Savior, Jesus, to them in the deepest of love for them.

One of the many promises of God that He has applied to me is that He has saved me. And now that I can see His glory and that He has bought me from the wages of my sin through the precious blood of Jesus and has put His Spirit within me, I now pray and ask the same for my family and trust Him that He will save my family of today and for generations to come as He has so declared.

The LORD your God will circumcise your heart and the heart of your offspring, so that you will love the LORD your God with all your heart and with all your soul, that you may live. (Deut. 30:6)

Father, thank You for who You are, for Your glory now being revealed within my heart, and I pray that You will continue to save the family You have made me a part of for generations to come!

In Jesus's name I ask, amen!

Let us begin.

Acknowledgments

Have you ever noticed how traditional birthday cards are written? Most, if not all, are written from the perspective of the giver of the card and not to the receiver of the card.

For example, here is how many are written.
Front Cover:

> Happy Birthday to You.

Inside Cover:

> Happy Birthday to someone special, who makes
> ME feel so Loved and Appreciated.

> May your day be bright.

Then you sign it:

> All my love, XXXOOO

I say this to say that it is hard not to be self-focused. For some reason, we like to be in the center of attention. But when you write a book, I am learning that it is even harder not to say "I." For I so want to be anonymous behind Jesus, my Lord and Savior, for He is so worthy! But in that He uses people to fulfill the counsel of His will doing life with other people, and it is valuable to identify those for whom Christ is also working in within this endeavor—which I sense being called to do and the Lord now bringing folks along to help.

God is so BIG! All the things He does, He planned, and He created, for His glory and our enjoyment in Him and how it all fits together, just amazes me! And He is never busy, never tired, never torn between this or that—what a GREAT God we serve!

I want to thank God for who He is, and then the people He has brought to help me to worship Him in life together for this moment.

To My Lord and Savior

Take a moment to imagine you were there when Jesus walked the earth some two thousand years ago. Imagine you were there when on the hill where He preached the Sermon on the Mount, or that you were there when He was in a home, when suddenly the crowd cut a big hole in the roof of the house and they lowered down a sick man to see Jesus speaking! Or you were in the back of the boat when Peter stepped out onto the water to walk to Jesus. Jesus is real. History has been foretold and, in part, now written to the times of Jesus's life two thousand years ago.

Wow! And now not only did He come to live a perfect life, and then unjustly die a cruel death at the hands of sinful men, He came to save that which was lost, to the perfect will of God the Father! And to that, life is all about and for Jesus! Thank You, Jesus, for saving me and for Your Spirit now being within me, through salvation given to me though the will of the Father, by Your works of salvation in obedience to the will of the Father toward me, by the Holy Spirit testifying to me.

Thank You, Jesus, for all that You are and for guiding me as I study, as I write, and as I think upon Your glory!

To My Wife and Family, for Whom the Lord Has Blessed Me

I thank God for blessing me with such a wonderful wife, Sandy, for her patience and support all throughout our marriage. She has been such a blessing. How God uses marriage to showcase how He loves us becomes more evident each day as our love grows together in Christ and for each other through Christ!

And for my entire family, who have allowed me to practice and make mistakes in life toward them and for the love they have given back in return.

To my family, I love you!

To Those for Whom I Sat under throughout My Life That God Used to Teach Me His Word and to Instruct Me in Application

This could be a long attribution. For God has placed so many people within my life—learning about God since He called me into His Son. Many books on my shelf would be a start. I will limit myself to those whom I remember best, but please know there are many others that God used and still uses to mold the gift of salvation within me.

Pastors, Teachers, and Friends

As I read the Bible, and sit under various pastors, and read, listen, and watch various pastors/teachers of the word, here are a few men whom God has used to open my understanding to Himself that I want to acknowledge!

In my early married days of walking in faith, God brought my family to a Baptist church through my wife's church background, and in that I sat under good local teachers of the Gospel.

I want to thank God for first bringing Sandy and me to Bible Baptist Church and to Pastor Bob Stamp. God used Bob to start shaping the foundation of the Gospel knowledge within our home. Through BBC, when we started our family, God gave Bob the vision and leadership to bring the gospel message to the local community through preaching, teaching, and even music and that all benefited our family as a "remembrance stone of faith" for us.

And from there, I want to next thank God for Pastor John Buchta, who was called to BBC as their next pastor. John came with a strong doctrinal approach but was only at BBC for a few years, when God quickly called him home after cancer was discovered. But while John was there, God used him to open the scriptures to the deeper parts of the "theological pool" for me, and through John, I learned to "own" what I believe.

Now this season lasted for many years of relationship within one body of believers—way over twenty years there, but in God's will and timing—God then called us out from within this fellowship to attend another Baptist fellowship about twenty-five miles away, led by Pastor Dave Maitland, or PD as he is affectionately known.

It is within this church that God used PD to teach us about love. God brought us here to see how to love as Christ loves, and it is through PD's leadership God taught us love in such a deeper sense of the word.

And I might also add faith too, for within this season of life for us, God allowed a big trial to hit our home, and God used PD to not only teach us about love and faith but also to be a living example to it. Looking back, I can now see God not only moving us to this church but now for the reasons why He did—to give us comfort through the storm for the time there—and I praise God for His grace and mercy He has given us and for the love and courage He gave PD to share with us.

Which brings us to today. God again led us to move back to a church closer to home about seven years ago with a much larger fellowship into the thousands—under the direction of Pastor Matt Kaltenberger.

Matt is the son-in-law of Bob Stamp, and God has used Matt by starting a new church about twenty years ago. God has blessed this fellowship through its approach to reaching folks who are "searching for God" and not a church. We believe that God has brought us here to learn more about grace in fellowship and to use what He has prepared us for over the last thirty-nine years of our marriage to be used within this fellowship.

It is interesting to look back to see what God is doing with us and toward us. God has used these pastors to prepare us to be a mission within our home, workplace, and neighborhoods, and I thank God for their service and their love of Jesus and for us.

I also want to acknowledge God using contemporary national and global ministries of John MacArthur, John Piper, R.C. Sproul, J. Vernon McGee, and Alistair Begg, to name a few, along with the authors of my bookshelf: of FF Bruce, JI Packer, Charles Spurgeon, and others. You will find as you read that I have a strong Reformed position, which is where I see the apostle Paul. To these men, I also thank God for their love of Christ and for using their gift of teaching and preaching that I have also learned from.

To Those Who Have Helped Me Pull This Book Together in Edits, Grammar, Content, and Theological Validation

I so appreciate these men in their selflessness to review my heart through my writings. I never learned how to type, so with my two index fingers chasing after my thoughts, not only are they dealing with what I am thinking but also with the typos of my two-fingered typing. Add this to spelling errors, auto-check errors, wrong form of the word, words ahead of another, theological clarification, and grammar, these brothers in Christ have been such a blessing in helping me to be clearer in thought and in writing "more better."

A big thanks to Dr. James Hugg, who was a big early help with proofing my grammar and corralling my train of thought and for the mutual times of study between us and for his support in prayer. What a blessing you are in your support and fellowship!

And thanking God for Don Lind, a former business associate of mine for whom when we were in the office together, we always seemed to focus more on the Lord in our conversations and not the job of the moment. It is comforting and a blessing having "church" anywhere. I so thank God for Don's insight to help me keep it real for the reader's understanding and also for his testimony of Christ.

Along with thanking God for bringing James and Don into my life, I want to thank Pastor Matt Kaltenberger for his friendship and support and for meeting at breakfast every quarter as we worship, pray, and explore the doctrines of our faith in the deeper parts of the pool.

I also want to thank my parents, Bernie and Marjorie Rosen, who are now with our Lord and Savior. I treasure the sweet times of fellowship with them as God was moving them from life to life, for which I will always cherish. And also for my sister Barb and her faith and walk with our Lord too. What a blessing now realized to the call of God within our home during the 1970s.

And lastly, I also want to acknowledge my mother-in-law, Nola Walker-Gramnola, for whom I have always admired her faith from a distance. She has had a very tough life, and yet her faith has never wavered. She is a quiet and private person, but she was the first person who read my manuscript from cover to cover within two days, and I had a Post-it note stuck to the front cover with such encouraging feedback in return. Not only do I thank God for her being the mother of my wife, but I thank God for her strength of faith in life.

Introduction

Finding Rest in the Glory and Sovereignty of Our Lord

To God be the glory! As I study the Bible, I give God praise with thanksgiving for His immeasurable grace, mercies, and love that He has revealed to us through His word. That He calls and uses ordinary men to write His words within the Bible to both proclaim and reveal to man His glory, His holiness, His love, His character, His grace, His mercy, and His righteousness simply amazes me.

And even today, God still uses people to do His will. He uses preachers and teachers; missionaries and evangelists; even you and me, to facilitate, to bring about, and to accomplish His will through time.

Take today's churches for example: Many good Christ-proclaiming, Christ-believing churches have goals—to preach the gospel of salvation and to make disciples of Jesus. For Jesus tells His disciples in Matthew 28:19,

> Go therefore and make disciples of all nations, baptizing them in the name of the Father and of the Son and of the Holy Spirit, teaching them to observe all that I have commanded you. And behold, I am with you always, to the end of the age.

The shelves of my personal library are filled with excellent books written by good Christian men and women believers from various decades in support of learning about "ways" to become more like Jesus. In fact, there was a movement called WWJD—What Would Jesus Do—popular back in the '90s decade of the twentieth century. They also "marketed" wrist bands with those initials, and many wore them as a reminder to choose doing right over wrong.

I share this to say, that in being a "follower of Christ," doing what is right is our faithful service. But as a Christian, there must be more than just "following Jesus." More than just doing "what is right." And even more than loving God. Please hear my heart that I am not saying that the following, the serving, and the loving Jesus are not important. They truly are! What I am offering you to see is that the word of God above all declares the glory of God as the ultimate value to God, and that all things point back to God's glory.

It is God's working through Christ and the Holy Spirit within you and me as to our loving Him, as to our faith in belief, as to our now walk of obedience and service, and as to our security of His holding us as His possession to the glory of God.

The blinders of our eyes, now having been removed by the Holy Spirit to the light of the Gospel, Christ is radiantly bright to those who believe—bringing us into an awareness, an awe, of the glory of the Gospel of Christ. For now we see His glory as brightly visible through His word and work of Jesus Christ and ultimately the highest of desirability, and as God gives us repentance, gives us faith, removes the heart of stone and gives us a new heart of flesh with His love written all over it. By His Spirit living within us, we willingly, humbly, and gratefully fall down, and we worship Him—forever! (Big goose bumps excite me as I type this.)

> [And] I saw the Lord sitting upon a throne, high and lifted up; and the train of his robe filled the temple. Above him stood the seraphim. Each had six wings: with two he covered his face, and with two he covered his feet, and with two he flew. And one called to another and said: "Holy, holy,

holy is the LORD of hosts; the whole earth is full
of his glory!" (Isa. 6:1–3)

And in studying the Bible, God is revealing that being a disciple
is more than thinking what Jesus would do in a situation.

John 4:23 quickly comes to mind: "But the hour is coming,
and is now here, when the true worshipers will worship the Father
in spirit and truth, for the Father is seeking such people to worship
him."

Although obedience is especially important, for God does
declare that obedience is better than sacrifice, this motive, as I see it
through my studies, is not complete as God's main desire for us.

God's glory is the most important thing to God, and through
that, He works in His creation to the glory and counsel of His will.
As I will explain later, God's name, God's glory, and God's righteousness are the most valuable attributes of Himself to Himself, and there
is no one else who could offer anything that would satisfy these attributes except God Himself, through His Son, Jesus. Thus, He saves
us for His name's sake, and we cannot save ourselves by believing for
our own salvation's sake.

Jesus asks Peter, "Do you love me?" That, in my opinion, is the
better question to answer than "What would Jesus do?" For Jesus
challenges Peter to respond with love, and Peter replied to Jesus as
best he could, and yet Peter went back to fishing. Turn back a few
months and Peter saw Jesus's glory, when he was young in his relationship with Jesus while he was fishing:

> And when he had finished speaking, he said to
> Simon, "Put out into the deep and let down your
> nets for a catch." And Simon answered, "Master,
> we toiled all night and took nothing! But at your
> word I will let down the nets." And when they
> had done this, they enclosed a large number
> of fish, and their nets were breaking. They sig-
> naled to their partners in the other boat to come
> and help them. And they came and filled both

the boats, so that they began to sink. But when Simon Peter saw it, **he fell down at Jesus' knees, saying, "Depart from me, for I am a sinful man, O Lord."** (Luke 5:4–8)

But now notice how after Jesus's resurrection, that Jesus opened the disciple's minds to understand that all the scriptures were about Him:

> Then he said to them, "These are my words that I spoke to you while I was still with you, that everything written about me in the Law of Moses and the Prophets and the Psalms must be fulfilled." Then he opened their minds to understand the Scriptures. (Luke 24:44–45)

Who Peter now boldly proclaims:

> For we did not follow cleverly devised myths when we made known to you the power and coming of our Lord Jesus Christ, but we were eyewitnesses of his majesty. For when he received honor and glory from God the Father, and the voice was borne to him by the Majestic Glory, "This is my beloved Son, with whom I am well pleased." (2 Pet. 1:16–17)

God's glory!

From there all things fit together. For and toward the glory of God, all things work together, according to the counsel of His will.

All of creation. For the glory of God! All things actively working together according to the counsel of His will. For the glory of God! The sin that is. Yes, for the glory of God! Our lives and salvation, for the glory of God.

One of the chapters I will present deals with man's salvation. In part, the Bible declares that salvation is of the Lord. And to explain in summarization, salvation of man is for God, of God, by God, in God, through God, because of God, and for the Glory of God, lest any man would boast. As Jesus is the just and the justifier, He is also the author and finisher of our faith.

This book is my attempt to show the sovereignty of God within us—for His name's sake, for His glory to be treasured and cherished. For by His Spirit living in us, we can now see Christ as our Lord, our Savior, and to see His glory forever and ever.

It is God who created me; it is God who sought me for salvation as part of the bride of Christ; it is God who wrote my name within the book of life; it is God who saved me; it is God who redeems me; it is God now living within me; it is God who won my battle with alcohol; it is God who protects me daily from sinning into unbelief; it is God who works the good works He has called me to walk in; it is God who gives wisdom and understanding; it is God who changes a heart, my heart; it is God who has sanctified me; it is God who keeps me; it is God who justifies me; and it is God who glorifies me, all through and for Jesus, His Son and my Lord and Savior. It is all God!

However, the sin I still do is not caused by God making me sin (Jas. 1:13) but of me. Call it a sin hangover. Every good gift is from God, and every sinful action is still from me, for the flesh is weak. The difference now is that God has opened the eyes of my heart to the awareness of sin and now to a relationship, one of love and submission to Jesus our Lord and Savior, to humbly confess my sin to the Father who loves me through His Son Jesus. I now no longer "practice" the sins of my past, for I now humbly see that Christ has died for all my sins, and He blesses me with the wisdom of responding in repentance, faith, and love. HOWEVER, God does use our sin in His plan and purpose to the counsel of His will, i.e., Genesis 50:20. As for you, you meant evil against me, but God meant it for good, to bring it about that many people should be kept alive, as they are today.

If there is one message I can leave with you, as Jesus teaches us, it would be to love the Lord your God with all your heart, mind, and soul. Seek to glorify God in all you do and look upon His glory as your most valuable possession.

And as seriously as I can type, the glory of Christ and your love of Him is the most important treasure you will ever possess, and if He is yours today, I praise God for His working within your heart. And if you are not there yet with Him, I pray with you and for you and ask God to glorify Himself through revealing to you His love for you in a way that you will understand the wisdom of His salvation directed toward you.

There is nothing to hold you back, for if you

> Confess with your mouth that Jesus is Lord and believe in your heart that God raised him from the dead, you will be saved. For with the heart one believes and is justified, and with the mouth one confesses and is saved. For the Scripture says, "Everyone who believes in him will not be put to shame." For there is no distinction between Jew and Greek; for the same Lord is Lord of all, bestowing his riches on all who call on him. For **"everyone who calls on the name of the Lord will be saved**." (Rom. 10:9–13)

Tribute

To my Lord and Savior, Jesus Christ. I am so unworthy. So unworthy of the grace of God in salvation, so unworthy to even think I can write a book, let alone a book about my Lord and Savior and about how to better understand His love and His grace toward you and me as part of His glory unto Himself.

Thank you, Jesus! Thank you for saving me! Thank you for your patience with me. Thank you for your loving me. Thank you for your forgiveness of all my sins. Thank you for dying for me in payment for all my sins. Thank you for your glory, which in John 17 you pray that I will see one day face-to-face. Thank you for your grace. Thank you for your mercy. And thank you for your holiness and righteousness. Thank you for leading me, for keeping me, and for protecting me. And in my appreciation, I replace the thank-you with praises. All glory, praise, and honor to you, my Lord, my Savior, and my King!

Testimony

Even as I type this, my eyes well up with tears in remembrance of His mercy and grace He has bestowed upon me and my family in His saving us.

Going back to a summer night in August of 1971, just turning fourteen and being at a church camp in Northeastern Ohio, a local Pittsburgh radio DJ turned part-time evangelist preached the Gospel of Jesus to a bunch of church kids, and it was that night the miracle of the Holy Spirit working in my heart and in conjunction working in and through this DJ's words of presenting the Gospel that I believed the gospel of Jesus, repented from my sinfulness, and was adopted as a child of God that night.

What makes this more important to me is that I grew up in church. My father was from a large Roman Catholic family, being the twelfth child of thirteen and having lost both parents early in his life; and my mother, having an older sister of four years, being raised Episcopalian, for her mother, sister, and father arrived to the USA from England in around 1929, and, well, they were British, thus having the Church of England as their legacy.

And with my dad loving my mom deeply, it was easy for him to adapt my mom's religious background—close enough to being RC—and thus he took us to an Episcopal church every Sunday, and we became involved within the Episcopal church. And with that, I was raised going to the local Episcopal church and learned the doctrines of the church with all its creeds and traditions.

I was confirmed in the church at twelve years old, became an acolyte to the priest's service, was awarded the Bishop's Award for being a "top" acolyte, and thought I was very good and holy at that time. Thinking that church doctrine and the traditions of the church gave me reason that I was okay with God, that as a young teen I began to wander into drinking alcohol and smoking cigarettes—which were not "really sins," I thought.

And as a young teen, I also had a need to be accepted by the circle of friends I had at the time. For I also wanted to be liked by my friends, and thus, this behavior became important at this stage of my life. I thought I had both God's and my friends' approval. In my mind, I had the best of both worlds: partying on Friday and Saturday, church on Sunday. It was a good life at the time, or so I thought.

Thus in 1970, I was given the opportunity to go to this same church camp the previous year when I was thirteen, and being my first time there, I heard the same Gospel message preached as when I was fourteen, and thought then, I am already a Christian. I thought, "I know who Jesus is. I know that He is my Savior, for He died for the sins of the whole world. I, being part of the world and part of the church and a servant of the church as an acolyte, am already 'in.'"

"This must be for the other kids who did not have a church background." With that in my mind, the Gospel was preached, I assumed it was for the other kids there who did not know about Jesus, so I went out and found a girlfriend and had a great week at camp.

Thus, when next year rolled around, and remembering that I found a girlfriend for the week the year prior, I said, "Sign me up!" I went looking for another opportunity to meet another girl, but instead Jesus met with me.

To say my life has changed is an understatement, to the point that this change is still happening even to this day. The love of Christ is deeper and fuller than any earthy relationship anyone could experience, and it is through Christ I am what I am, not perfect yet, but forgiven and loved.

It is through and because of Christ that among the many blessings He has given me since that night, He has blessed me with my own family and with the grace given me in my life seeing His hand in leading me along the way, to the glory of God! Through that, He has blessed me with a wonderful Christ-believing wife, Sandy, having just celebrated our thirty-ninth year of marriage. God has used her in so many ways for me to learn more about Himself and about true love, grace, and patience He has with me. She truly is a gift of God to help me grow in Christ, and her love of Jesus first and then for me and the family is truly a blessing.

And now that our two children have grown, Christopher and Ashley, seeing God calling both to faith and both having to deal with their own different pains in life and seeing God's hand, in as much as with me, leading them through it has also been a blessing. I praise God for them and pray that God would continue His working in their lives so that they seek His glory more each day.

And with Ashley seeing God bringing Nicholas, a Christ-believing husband beginning as high school sweethearts, who are walking in faith together that God has prepared for them, is a big answer to prayer and a blessing to Sandy and me.

God's blessed them with four daughters, our granddaughters, and just thinking about them makes me smile and praise God for them. Needless to say, we are praying for God to grant them salvation as well. What a blessing being a grandfather is to Hailey Grace, Aubrey Rose, Savannah Kate, and Olivia Claire!

There is so much more to declare in between the lines that deal with how God has worked within our lives regarding faith, health, career, trials, blessings, safety, etc. that I could add, but refrain, for this would be my story and not Christ's

An old hymn declares "To God be the glory, great things He hath Done," which sums up what I hope and trust to convey in writing what follows.

Father, I pray that I can faithfully and accurately write what you are laying upon my heart from the scriptures to learn and study from, and if it's your will that this also becomes teaching for others to learn and grow from, that You will receive the glory and honor from us both, me and each reader.

Father, what a comfort it is to know that You are sovereign in all things, and Your revealed will within Your word is as a sliver of wisdom to us that only You can convey the understandings to our hearts and minds. I pray that the Holy Spirit will enable me and those who may read this to see Your glory, rest in Your comfort, and enjoy all that You are in this life and in eternity as You have planned and prepared. I ask this in my Lord and Savior's name, Jesus Christ. Amen.

The Sovereignty of God in Our Daily Lives through the Field of Scripture

My thought to this section is to reorder a few scriptures that have spoken to my heart toward God's glory in His sovereign grace toward me, before I write and share my understandings.

If I do this correctly, I hope to show the sovereignty of God from the new covenant through the second coming by reordering scripture alone, using a "cliff notes" of scripture style, if you will. For this is my attempt to first let scripture interpret scripture, so that my humanness does not get in the way.

To these scriptures, I've added a few guiding comments here and there that you will see by it having [brackets] around them or having underlines, bolded, or italicized words or phrases that I've pulled out from my studies over the years, just to share what God has impressed upon my heart in His teaching me through my studies.

Try reading this next section first, and also try to read it a few times before moving on, to let the Word surround you and envelop you, asking the Holy Spirit to give you wisdom and understanding before you travel further (Jas. 1:5). It would thrill my heart if you and God sat down and just read the scriptures together, soaking in His majesty and glory as the scriptures speak to your heart through His Spirit guiding your way. For this would be the better course of study.

And with my rereading these verses now as I type, I am compelled by His Spirit to pray and thank the Lord again for His Word, for His glory, for His comfort, and for His grace toward me. Lord, may those who read Your words that now follow be also blessed by You as You have so blessed me. It is in Jesus's name I ask, amen!

> Then the Lord said to me, "You have seen well, for <u>I am watching over my word to perform it</u>." (Jer. 1:12)

> Behold, the days are coming, declares the Lord, when **I will** make a new covenant with the house of Israel and the house of Judah, not like the covenant that **I made** with their fathers on the day when **I took** them by the hand to bring them out of the land of Egypt, my covenant that they broke, though **I was** their husband, declares the Lord. <u>For this is the covenant that **I will** make with the house of Israel after those days</u>, declares the Lord: **I will** put my law within them, and **I will** write it on their hearts. And **I will** be their God, and they shall be my people. (Jer. 31:31–33)

[Notice how many **I will** statements God says and how no "man's will" statements there are. Stay tuned, more to be said later.]

> And he took bread, and when he had given thanks, he broke it and gave it to them, saying, "This is <u>my body, which is given for you</u>. Do this in remembrance of me." And likewise the cup after they had eaten, saying, "<u>This cup that is poured out for you is the new covenant in my blood</u>." (Luke 22:19–20)

> In the same way also he took the cup, after supper, saying, "<u>This cup is the new covenant in my blood</u>. Do this, as often as you drink it, in remembrance of me." (1 Cor. 11:25)

THE SOVEREIGNTY OF GOD IN OUR DAILY LIVES

Are we beginning to commend ourselves again? Or do we need, as some do, letters of recommendation to you, or from you? You yourselves are our letter of recommendation, written on our hearts, to be known and read by all. And you show that you are a letter from Christ delivered by us, written not with ink but with the Spirit of the living God, not on tablets of stone but on tablets of human hearts. Such is the confidence that we have through Christ toward God. Not that we are sufficient in ourselves to claim anything as coming from us, but our sufficiency is from God, who has made us sufficient to be ministers of a new covenant, not of the letter but of the Spirit. For the letter kills, but the Spirit gives life. (2 Cor. 3:1–6)

But as it is, Christ has obtained a ministry that is as much more excellent than the old as the covenant he mediates is better, since it is enacted on better promises. For if that first covenant had been faultless, there would have been no occasion to look for a second. For he finds fault with them when he says: "*Behold, the days are coming, declares the Lord, when I will establish a new covenant with the house of Israel and with the house of Judah, not like the covenant that I made with their fathers on the day when I took them by the hand to bring them out of the land of Egypt.* For they did not continue in my covenant, and so I showed no concern for them, declares the Lord. *For this is the covenant that I will make with the house of Israel after those days, declares the Lord: I will put my laws into their minds, and write them on their hearts, and I will be their God, and they shall be my people.*" (Heb. 8:6–10)

But it is not as though the word of God has failed. For not all who are descended from Israel belong to Israel, and not all are children of Abraham because they are his offspring, but "Through Isaac shall your offspring be named." <u>This means that it is not the children of the flesh who are the children of God, but the children of the promise are counted as offspring</u>. (Rom. 9:6–8)

Therefore he [Jesus] is the mediator of a new covenant, <u>so that those who are called</u> may receive the promised eternal inheritance, since a death has occurred that redeems them from the transgressions committed under the first covenant. (Heb. 9:15)

<u>And **I** will give you a new heart, and a new spirit **I** will put within you. And **I** will remove the heart of stone from your flesh and give you a heart of flesh. And **I** will put my Spirit within you, and cause you to walk in my statutes and be careful to obey my rules</u>. (Ezek. 36:26–27)

But this is what was uttered through the prophet Joel: "And in the last days it shall be, God declares, that I will pour out my Spirit on all flesh, and your sons and your daughters shall prophesy, and your young men shall see visions, and your old men shall dream dreams; even on my male servants and female servants in those days I will pour out my Spirit, and they shall prophesy." (Acts 2:16–18)

The Lord Will Pour Out His Spirit: "And it shall come to pass afterward, that I will pour out my Spirit on all flesh; your sons and your daughters shall prophesy, your old men shall dream dreams, and your young men shall see visions. Even on the male and female servants in those days I will pour out my Spirit." (Joel 2:28–29)

The LORD your God will circumcise your heart and the heart of your offspring, so that you will love the LORD your God with all your heart and with all your soul, that you may live. (Deut. 30:6)

Everyone who believes **that Jesus is the Christ has been born of God,** and everyone who loves the Father loves whoever has been born of him. (1 John 5:1)

But to all who did **receive him, who believed in his name,** he gave the right to become children of God, who were born, not of blood nor of the will of the flesh nor of the will of man, but of God. (John 1:12–13)

[To receive Jesus is to believe in His name. When one receives Christ, what they should understand is that they miraculously have come to believe in Christ. And this belief—faith—is not a human effort (also see Ephesians 2:8–9); it is God-breathed, a spirit-born action not of the flesh but of God. I develop this further within the first chapter and "The Building Is on Fire" analogy.]

But those that were sown on the good soil are the ones who hear the word and accept it [believe] and bear fruit, thirtyfold and sixtyfold and a hundredfold. (Mark 4:20)

[Receiving or accepting Jesus = Believing in Jesus. I will develop this further in Chapters 1 and 2. Also of importance is the reference to "the good soil." What or who make this soil "good"?]

[The following section of scriptures details God's "calling, choosing, and electing" folks to the power of the Gospel—shining the glory of Christ into the heart of the new believer for them to "accept, receive, and believe" the Gospel of salvation. This list is but a sample.]

> And he said to them, "To you has been given the secret of the kingdom of God, but for those outside everything is in parables, so that 'they may indeed see but not perceive, and may indeed hear but not understand, lest they should turn and be forgiven.'" (Mark 4:11–12)

> And when the Gentiles heard this, they began rejoicing and glorifying the word of the Lord, and as many as were appointed to eternal life believed. (Acts 13:48)

> For consider your calling, brothers: not many of you were wise according to worldly standards, not many were powerful, not many were of noble birth. But God chose what is foolish in the world to shame the wise; God chose what is weak in the world to shame the strong; God chose what is low and despised in the world, even things that are not, to bring to nothing things that are, so that no human being might boast in the presence of God. *And because of him you are in Christ Jesus, who became to us wisdom from God, righteousness and sanctification and redemption, so that, as it is written, "Let the one who boasts, boast in the Lord."* (1 Cor. 1:26–31)

> O foolish Galatians! Who has bewitched you? It was before your eyes that Jesus Christ was publicly portrayed as crucified. Let me ask you only

this: <u>Did you receive the Spirit by works of the law or by hearing with faith?</u> Are you so foolish? Having begun by the Spirit, are you now being perfected by the flesh? Did you suffer so many things in vain—if indeed it was in vain? <u>Does he who supplies the Spirit to you and works miracles among you do so by works of the law, or by hearing with faith—just as Abraham "believed God, and it was counted to him as righteousness"? Know then that it is those of faith who are the sons of Abraham.</u> And the Scripture, <u>foreseeing that God would justify the Gentiles by faith, preached the gospel beforehand to Abraham, saying, "In you shall all the nations be blessed." So then, those who are of faith are blessed along with Abraham, the man of faith.</u> (Gal. 3:1–9)

For even the Son of Man came not to be served but to serve, and **to give his life as a ransom for many**. (Mark 10:45)

[For many, and not for all? Who then are the many? They are all who believe. Who will believe? All that the Spirit wills.]

The wind blows where it wishes, and you hear its sound, but you do not know where it comes from or where it goes. So it is with everyone who is born of the Spirit. (John 3:8)

For **by grace** you have been saved **through faith**. And this **is not your own doing**; it is the **gift of God**, not a result of works, **so that no one may boast**. For we are his workmanship, **<u>created in Christ Jesus for good works, which God prepared beforehand, that we should walk in</u>**

them. [The gift of God is grace and faith.] (Eph. 2:8–10)

For he says to Moses, "I will have mercy on whom I have mercy, and I will have compassion on whom I have compassion." [**So then it depends not on human will or exertion, but on God**, who has mercy.] (Rom. 9:15–16)

But we ought always to give thanks to God for you, brothers beloved by the Lord, because **God chose you as the firstfruits to be saved**, through sanctification by the Spirit and belief in the truth. (2 Thess. 2:13)

For we are God's handiwork, created in Christ Jesus to do good works, which God prepared in advance for us to do. Ephesians 2:10

All things have been committed to me by my Father. No one knows the Son except the Father, and no one knows the Father except the Son and those to whom the Son chooses to reveal him. (Matt. 11:27)

[Having the blinders of sin now being removed, we should now see God's word showing us that He is actively working within us. The more we read and renew our mind with His word, the more God reveals to us and enables our understanding of the wonder of His grace, mercy, and treasure of Christ.]

For it is God who works in you to will and to act in order to fulfill his good purpose. (Phil. 2:13)

But by the grace of God I am what I am, and his grace to me was not without effect. No, I worked harder than all of them—yet not I, but the grace of God that was with [in] me. (1 Cor. 15:10)

Now may the God of peace, who through the blood of the eternal covenant brought back from the dead our Lord Jesus, that great Shepherd of the sheep, equip you with everything good for doing his will, and may he work in us what is pleasing to him, through Jesus Christ, to whom be glory for ever and ever. Amen. (Heb. 13:20–21)

Therefore I want you to understand that no one speaking in the Spirit of God ever says "Jesus is accursed!" and no one can say "Jesus is Lord" except in the Holy Spirit. (1 Cor. 12:3)

[This is a powerful truth…a quick self-evidence to those who are wondering if they are saved. It is the Holy Spirit within us that gives us the words, the faith, and the understandings that Jesus is Lord indeed!]

The plans of the heart belong to man, but the answer of the tongue is from the LORD. (Proverbs 16:1)

Nathanael said to him, "Can anything good come out of Nazareth?" Philip said to him, "Come and see." Jesus saw Nathanael coming toward him and said of him, "Behold, an Israelite indeed, in whom there is no deceit!" Nathanael said to him, "How do you know me?" Jesus answered him, "Before Philip called you, when you were under the fig tree, I saw you." Nathanael answered him, "Rabbi, you are the Son of God! You are the King of Israel!" Jesus answered him, "Because I said to you, 'I saw you under the fig tree,' do you

believe? You will see greater things than these."
(John 1:46–50)

In their hearts humans plan their course, but the
Lord establishes their steps. (Prov. 16:9)

The lot is cast into the lap, but its every decision
is from the Lord. (Prov. 16:33)

As for you, my son Solomon, know the God of
your father, and serve Him with a whole heart and
a willing mind; for the LORD searches all hearts,
and understands every intent of the thoughts.
If you seek Him, He will let you find Him; but
if you forsake Him, He will reject you forever.
Consider now, for the LORD has chosen you to
build a house for the sanctuary; be courageous
and act. (1 Chron. 28:9–10)

He makes me lie down in green pastures; He leads
me beside quiet waters. He restores my soul; He
guides me in the paths of righteousness For His
name's sake. (Ps. 23:2–3)

For You are my rock and my fortress; For Your
name's sake You will lead me and guide me. (Ps.
31:3)

There is nothing better for a person than that he
should eat and drink and find enjoyment in his
toil. This also, I saw, is from the hand of God.
(Eccles. 2:24)

Thus says the LORD, your Redeemer, the Holy
One of Israel, "I am the LORD your God, who

teaches you to profit, Who leads you in the way you should go." (Isa. 48:17)

I know, O LORD, that a man's way is not in himself, Nor is it in a man who walks to direct his steps. (Jer. 10:23)

The heart is deceitful above all things, and desperately sick; who can understand it? "I the LORD search the heart and test the mind, to give every man according to his ways, according to the fruit of his deeds." (Jer. 17:9–10)

For he will be great before the Lord. And he must not drink wine or strong drink, and <u>he will be filled with the Holy Spirit, even from his mother's womb.</u> (Luke 1:15)

[John the Baptist is the only person that I know of who is filled with the Holy Spirit ("born again") while growing within his mother, Elizabeth.]

Simon Peter, a servant and apostle of Jesus Christ, To those who have obtained a faith of equal standing with ours by the righteousness of our God and Savior Jesus Christ: <u>May grace and peace be multiplied to you **in the knowledge of God and of Jesus our Lord.**</u> (2 Peter 1:1–2)

[Paul's and Peter's prayers show us that God enables us with wisdom and knowledge, as James also writes.]

In him you also are being built together into a dwelling place for God by the Spirit. (Ephesians 2:22)

And so, from the day we heard, <u>we have not ceased to pray for you, asking</u> **that you may be filled with the knowledge of his will in all spiritual wisdom and understanding**, so as to walk in a manner worthy of the Lord, fully pleasing to him: bearing fruit in every good work and **increasing in the knowledge of God;** being strengthened with all power, according to his glorious might, for all endurance and patience with joy; **giving thanks to the Father, who has qualified you** to share in the inheritance of the saints in light. (Colossians 1:9–12)

And you, who were dead in your trespasses and the uncircumcision of your flesh, **God made alive together with him**, having forgiven us all our trespasses. (Col. 2:13)

You are the Lord, **the God who chose Abram** and brought him out of Ur of the Chaldeans and gave him the name Abraham. (Neh. 9:7)

In their case the god of this world has blinded the minds of the unbelievers, to keep them from seeing the light of the gospel of the glory of Christ, who is the image of God. For what we proclaim is not ourselves, but Jesus Christ as Lord, with ourselves as your servants for Jesus' sake. For God, who said, "Let light shine out of darkness," has shone in our hearts to give the light of the knowledge of the glory of God in the face of Jesus Christ. (2 Cor. 4:4–6)

The natural person does not accept the things of the Spirit of God, for they are folly to him, and he is not able to understand them because they are spiritually discerned. (1 Cor. 2:14)

Jesus answered him, **"Truly, truly, I say to you, unless one is born again he cannot see the kingdom of God."** Nicodemus said to him, "How can a man be born when he is old? Can he enter a second time into his mother's womb and be born?" Jesus answered, **"Truly, truly, I say to you, unless one is born of water and the Spirit, he cannot enter the kingdom of God. That which is born of the flesh is flesh, and that which is born of the Spirit is spirit. Do not marvel that I said to you, 'You must be born again.' The wind blows where it wishes, and you hear its sound, but you do not know where it comes from or where it goes. So it is with everyone who is born of the Spirit."** (John 3:3–8)

[**Order of salvation: Born again first then belief**, not believing first then God makes you born again.]

And because you are sons, <u>God has sent the Spirit of his Son into our hearts</u>, crying, "Abba! Father!" So you are no longer a slave, but a son, and if a son, then an heir through God. (Gal. 4:6–7)

Paul, an apostle of Christ Jesus **by the will of God**, To the saints who are in Ephesus, and are faithful in Christ Jesus. (Eph. 1:1)

Paul, an apostle—not from men nor through man, **but through Jesus Christ and God the Father**, who raised him from the dead—and all the brothers who are with me, To the churches of Galatia: Grace to you and peace from God our Father and the Lord Jesus Christ. (Gal. 1:1–3)

But the Lord said to him [Ananias], "Go, **for he [Saul/Paul] is a chosen instrument of mine to carry my name before the Gentiles and kings and the children of Israel. For I will show him how much he must suffer for the sake of my name.**" So Ananias departed and entered the house. And laying his hands on him he said, "Brother Saul, the Lord Jesus who appeared to you on the road by which you came has sent me so that you may regain your sight and be filled with the Holy Spirit." (Acts 9:15–17)

But I will come to you soon, **if the Lord wills**, and I will find out not the talk of these arrogant people but their power. (1 Cor. 4:19)

For I would have you know, brothers, that the gospel that was preached by me is not man's gospel. For I did not receive it from any man, nor was I taught it, but I received it through a revelation of Jesus Christ. For you have heard of my former life in Judaism, how I persecuted the church of God violently and tried to destroy it. And I was advancing in Judaism beyond many of my own age among my people, so extremely zealous was I for the traditions of my fathers. **But when he who had set me apart before I was born, and who called me by his grace, was pleased to reveal his Son to me, in order that I might preach him among the Gentiles,** I did not immediately consult with anyone; nor did I go up to Jerusalem to those who were apostles before me, but I went away into Arabia, and returned again to Damascus. (Galatians 1:11–17)

Even **as he chose us in him before the foundation of the world**, that we should be holy and blameless before him. In love **he predestined us for adoption to himself as sons through Jesus Christ, according to the purpose of his will, to the praise of his glorious grace**, with which he has blessed us in the Beloved. (Eph. 1:4–6)

In him we have obtained an inheritance, **having been predestined according to the purpose of him who works all things according to the counsel of his will**, so that we who were the first to hope in Christ might be **to the praise of his glory**. (Eph. 1:11–12)

That the God of our Lord Jesus Christ, the Father of glory, **may give you the Spirit of wisdom and of revelation in the knowledge of him, having the eyes of your hearts enlightened**, that you may know what is the hope to which he has called you, what are the riches of his glorious inheritance in the saints, and what is the immeasurable greatness of his power toward us who believe, according to the working of his great might. (Eph. 1:17–19)

And we know that for those who love God all things work together for good, for those who are called according to his purpose. For those whom he <u>foreknew</u> **he also predestined to be conformed to the image of his Son,** in order that he might be the firstborn among many brothers. And **those whom he predestined he also called,** and **those whom he called he also justified**, and those **whom he justified he also glorified**. (Rom. 8:28–30)

[Will explain further within Chapter 6].

I thank God whom I serve, as did my ancestors, with a clear conscience, as I remember you constantly in my prayers night and day. As I remember your tears, I long to see you, that I may be filled with joy. I am reminded of your sincere faith, a faith that dwelt first in your grandmother Lois and your mother Eunice and now, I am sure, dwells in you as well. For this reason <u>I remind you to fan into flame the gift of God</u>, which is in you through the laying on of my hands, <u>for God gave us a spirit not of fear but of power and love and self-control</u>. (2 Tim. 1:3–7)

Therefore do not be ashamed of the testimony about our Lord, nor of me his prisoner, but share in suffering for the gospel by the power of God, [9] <u>who saved us and called us to a holy calling, not because of our works but because of his own purpose and grace, which he gave us in Christ Jesus before the ages began</u>, [10] and which **now has been manifested through the appearing of our Savior Christ Jesus, who abolished death and brought life and immortality to light through the gospel**. (2 Tim. 1:8–10)

For we are his workmanship, created in Christ Jesus for good works, which God prepared beforehand, that we should walk in them. (Ephesians 2:10 ESV)

All things have been handed over to me by my Father, and no one knows the Son except the Father, and no one knows the Father except the Son and anyone to whom the Son chooses to reveal him. (Matthew 11:27 ESV)

"Nevertheless, do not rejoice in this, that the spirits are subject to you, **but rejoice that your names are written in heaven.**" (Notice that Jesus tells them that your names are written in heaven. He also tells us in Revelation 13:8 about all the saints' names being written in the *Book of the Lamb who was slain,* which was written before the foundation of the world.) In that same hour he rejoiced in the Holy Spirit and said, "I thank you, Father, Lord of heaven and earth, that <u>you have hidden these things from the wise and understanding and revealed them to little children; yes, Father, for such was your gracious will.</u> All things have been handed over to me by my Father, and no one knows who the Son is except the Father, or who the Father is except the Son and anyone **to whom the Son chooses to reveal him.**" Then turning to the disciples he said privately, "Blessed are the eyes that see what you see! For I tell you that many prophets and kings desired to see what you see, and did not see it, and to hear what you hear, and did not hear it." (Luke 10:20–24)

Now when they drew near to Jerusalem, to Bethpage and Bethany, at the Mount of Olives, Jesus sent two of his disciples and said to them, "Go into the village in front of you, and immediately as you enter it you will find a colt tied, on which no one has ever sat. Untie it and bring it. If anyone says to you, 'Why are you doing this?'

say, 'The Lord has need of it and will send it back here immediately.'" And they went away and found a colt tied at a door outside in the street, and they untied it. And some of those standing there said to them, "What are you doing, untying the colt?" And they told them what Jesus had said, and they let them go. And they brought the colt to Jesus and threw their cloaks on it, and he sat on it. (Mark 11:1–7)

[See Chapter 7 for my comments.]

When it was evening, he reclined at the table with the twelve. And as they were eating, he said, "Truly, I say to you, one of you will betray me." And they were very sorrowful and began to say to him one after another, "Is it I, Lord?" He answered, "He who has dipped his hand in the dish with me will betray me. The Son of Man goes as it is written of him, but woe to that man by whom the Son of Man is betrayed! It would have been better for that man if he had not been born." Judas, who would betray him, answered, "Is it I, Rabbi?" He said to him, "You have said so." (Matthew 26:20–25; 31–35; 52–56)

[Here is my question to this discourse between Jesus and the twelve. When Jesus tells them—better yet, prophesies—about his upcoming betrayal, why does each disciple ask Jesus, "Is it I?"]

The apostle John helps to further clarify this within John 13:23–26:

One of his disciples, whom Jesus loved [that is John himself he is referring to], was reclining at table at Jesus' side, so Simon Peter motioned to him to ask Jesus of whom he was speaking. So that disciple, leaning back against Jesus, said to him, "Lord, who is it?" Jesus answered, "It is he to whom I will give this morsel of bread when I have dipped it." So when he had dipped the morsel, he gave it to Judas, the son of Simon Iscariot.

[Jesus even tells them it is the one who dips his hand in His dish with Him, prior to his dipping. Judas, in hearing this, why didn't he stop? If I was planning to do sin, and someone tells me my plan beforehand, wouldn't I have stopped? At least for the fear of being found out if not in repentance. The point here to see is that each man is accountable for his own actions, for in our unsaved hearts, we are blind to the truth of the gospel.]

Then Jesus said to them, "You will all fall away because of me this night. For it is written, 'I will strike the shepherd, and the sheep of the flock will be scattered.' But after I am raised up, I will go before you to Galilee." Peter answered him, "Though they all fall away because of you, I will never fall away." Jesus said to him, "Truly, I tell you, this very night, before the rooster crows, you will deny me three times." Peter said to him, "Even if I must die with you, I will not deny you!" And all the disciples said the same. (Matt. 26:31–35)

[Jesus continues to share what the future holds for Him as well for them. But look a bit deeper. It is not just as being God—knowing what the night will unfold as—but that it was written as scripture hundreds of years prior. And then back to tonight, He tells them after He "dies." He tells them to go to Galilee where he will meet with them again! And what did Peter hear? Only that Jesus will die. And then how did Jesus correct him? He personally tells Peter how he will respond to the night's activities against Jesus. Not only will you all be scattered, as it is written, but you, Peter, will deny me tonight!]

Then Jesus said to him, "Put your sword back into its place. For all who take the sword will perish by the sword. Do you think that I cannot appeal to my Father, and he will at once send me more than twelve legions of angels? But how then should the Scriptures be fulfilled, that it must be so?" At that hour Jesus said to the crowds, "Have you come out as against a robber, with swords and clubs to capture me? Day after day I sat in the temple teaching, and you did not seize me. But all this has taken place that the Scriptures of the prophets might be fulfilled." Then all the disciples left him and fled. (Matt. 26:52–56)

[And now in the thick of the night, Jesus is still teaching the scriptures, and, that He is fulfilling the scriptures before their eyes. For me this is very deep doctrine to the glory of God. See if you will—that Scripture foretells, Jesus now tells; and the government, the religious leaders, and the people are hearing Jesus, are seeing Jesus—live out the scriptures of His death foretold, and yet deaf to the scripture of Messiah come, blind to see that He is Jesus, and enjoying the sin of their own hearts.]

But **when God, who set me apart from my mother's womb and called me by his grace**, <u>was pleased to reveal his Son in me</u> so that I might preach him among the Gentiles, my immediate response was not to consult any human being. I did not go up to Jerusalem to see those who were apostles before I was, but I went into Arabia. Later I returned to Damascus. (Gal. 1:15–17)

Blessed be the God and Father of our Lord Jesus Christ! According to his great mercy, **he has caused us to be born again to a living hope through the resurrection of Jesus Christ from**

the dead, to an inheritance that is imperishable, undefiled, and unfading, kept in heaven for you, who by God's power are being guarded through faith for a salvation ready to be revealed in the last time. (1 Peter 1:3–5 ESV)

But you are a chosen race, a royal priesthood, a holy nation, a people for his own possession, that you may proclaim the excellencies of him **who called you out of darkness** into his marvelous light. Once you were not a people, but now you are God's people; once you had not received mercy, but now you have received mercy. (1 Peter 2:9–10)

Not that I have already obtained this or am already perfect, but I press on to make it my own, because Christ Jesus has made me his own. Brothers, I do not consider that I have made it my own. But one thing I do: forgetting what lies behind and straining forward to what lies ahead, I press on toward the goal for the prize of the upward call of God in Christ Jesus. Let those of us who are mature think this way, and if in anything you think otherwise, **God will reveal that also to you**. Only let us hold true to what we have attained. Brothers, join in imitating me, and keep your eyes on those who walk according to the example you have in us. (Phil. 3:12–17)

Every good gift and every perfect gift is from above, coming down from the Father of lights, with whom there is no variation or shadow due to change. Of his own will he brought us forth by the word of truth, that we should be a kind of firstfruits of his creatures. (Jas. 1:17–18)

For this reason I bow my knees before the Father, from whom every family in heaven and on earth is named, that according to the riches of his glory he may grant you to be strengthened with power through his Spirit in your inner being, so that Christ may dwell in your hearts through faith—that you, being rooted and grounded in love, may have strength to comprehend with all the saints what is the breadth and length and height and depth, and to know the love of Christ that surpasses knowledge, that you may be filled with all the fullness of God. Now to him who is able to do far more abundantly than all that we ask or think, according to the power at work within us, to him be glory in the church and in Christ Jesus throughout all generations, forever and ever. Amen. (Eph. 3:14–21)

And also for me, that words may be given to me in opening my mouth boldly to proclaim the mystery of the gospel, for which I am an ambassador in chains, that I may declare it boldly, as I ought to speak. (Ephesians 6:19–20)

For everyone who does wicked things hates the light and does not come to the light, lest his works should be exposed. But whoever does what is true comes to the light, so that it may be clearly seen that his works have been carried out in God." (John 3:20–21)

If any of you lacks wisdom, let him ask God, who gives generously to all without reproach, and it will be given him. (James 1:5)

Come now, you who say, "Today or tomorrow we will go into such and such a town and spend a year there and trade and make a profit—" yet you do not know what tomorrow will bring. What is your life? For you are a mist that appears for a little time and then vanishes. Instead you ought to say, "**If the Lord wills**, we will live and do this or that." (James 4:13–15)

And he said, "This is why I told you that no one can come to me unless it is granted him by the Father." (John 6:65)

For since, **in the wisdom of God**, the world did not know God through wisdom, it pleased God through the folly of what we preach to save those who believe. For Jews demand signs and Greeks seek wisdom, but we preach Christ crucified, a stumbling block to Jews and folly to Gentiles, but **to those who are called, both Jews and Greeks, Christ the power of God and the wisdom of God.** (1 Cor. 1:21–24)

One who heard us was a woman named Lydia, from the city of Thyatira, a seller of purple goods, who was a worshiper of God. **The Lord opened her heart to pay attention to what was said by Paul.** (Acts 16:14, ESV)

Perseverance

But do not overlook this one fact, beloved, that with the Lord one day is as a thousand years, and a thousand years as one day. The Lord is not slow to fulfill his promise as some count slowness, but is patient toward you, not wishing that any should perish, but that all should reach repentance. (2 Pet. 3:8–9)

[We shall discuss God's will and God's desire within Chapter 4.]

Have I any pleasure in the death of the wicked, declares the Lord God, and not rather that he should turn from his way and live? [The desire of God vs. the will of God] (Ezek. 18:23)

Now I would remind you, brothers, of the gospel I preached to you, which you received, in which you stand, and by which you are being saved, if you hold fast to the word I preached to you—unless you believed in vain. [Perseverance in faith is holding fast to Christ in the good works of obedience through faith, empowered by the Holy Spirit.] (1 Cor. 15:1–2)

And you, who once were alienated and hostile in mind, doing evil deeds, he [Christ] has now reconciled in his body of flesh by his death, in order to present you holy and blameless and above reproach before him, if indeed you continue in the faith, stable and steadfast, not shifting from the hope of the gospel that you heard, which has been proclaimed in all creation under heaven, and of which I, Paul, became a minister. (Col. 1:21–23)

Who desires all people to be saved and come to the knowledge of the truth. (1 Tim. 2:4)

[Another comparison that God desires all to be saved with those who are saved]

Compare to 2 Timothy 2:25–26:

> Opponents must be gently instructed, in the hope that God will grant them repentance leading them to a knowledge of the truth, and that they will come to their senses and escape from the trap of the devil, who has taken them captive to do his will. (NIV)

> But by the grace of God I am what I am, and his grace toward me was not in vain. On the contrary, I worked harder than any of them, though it was not I, but the grace of God that is with me. (1 Cor. 15:10)

> For the Lord will not cast off forever, but, <u>though he cause grief</u>, he will have compassion according to the abundance of his steadfast love; <u>for he does not afflict from his heart</u> or grieve the children of men. (Lam. 3:31–33)

> Or do you not know that the unrighteous will not inherit the kingdom of God? Do not be deceived: neither the sexually immoral, nor idolaters, nor adulterers, nor men who practice homosexuality, nor thieves, nor the greedy, nor drunkards, nor revilers, nor swindlers will inherit the kingdom of God. **And such were some of you. But you were washed, you were sanctified, you were justified in the name of the Lord Jesus Christ and by the Spirit of our God**. (1 Cor. 6:9–11)

> We know that we have passed out of death into life, because we love the brothers. Whoever does not love abides in death. Everyone who hates his brother is a murderer, and you know that no

murderer has eternal life abiding in him. (1 John 3:14–15)

So Jesus said to the Jews who had believed him, "If you abide in my word, you are truly my disciples, and you will know the truth, and the truth will set you free." (John 8:31–32)

[This call to action is genuine, but only if the spirit of God lives within you, for it is God who works within you for you to abide in His word.]

For the promise is for you and for your children and for all who are far off, everyone whom the Lord our God calls to himself." (Acts 2:39)

[I hang my hat on God's promises and continually pray through these scriptural promises for all my family and those I meet trusting God for their salvation and His glory!]

Concerning this salvation, the prophets who prophesied about the grace that was to be yours searched and inquired carefully, inquiring what person or time the Spirit of Christ in them was indicating when he predicted the sufferings of Christ and the subsequent glories. **It was revealed to them that they were serving not themselves but you**, in the things that have now been announced to you through those who preached the good news to you by the Holy Spirit sent from heaven, things into which angels long to look. (1 Peter 1:10–12)

What then is Apollos? What is Paul? Servants through whom you believed, as the Lord assigned to each. I planted, Apollos watered, but God gave the growth. So neither he who plants nor he who waters is anything, **but only God who gives the growth**. (1 Cor. 3:5–7)

Even as he chose us in him before the foundation of the world, that we should be holy and blameless before him. In love he predestined us for adoption to himself as sons through Jesus Christ, according to the purpose of his will, <u>to the praise of his glorious grace</u>, with which he has blessed us in the Beloved. In him we have redemption through his blood, the forgiveness of our trespasses, <u>according to the riches of his grace, which he lavished upon us, in all wisdom and insight making known to us the mystery of his will, according to his purpose, which he set forth in Christ</u>, as a plan for the fullness of time, to unite all things in him, things in heaven and things on earth. In him we have obtained an inheritance, having been predestined according to the purpose of him who works all things according to the counsel of his will. (Ephesians 1:4–11)

<u>Now to him who is able to keep you from stumbling</u> and to present you blameless before the presence of his glory with great joy, to the only God, our Savior, through Jesus Christ our Lord, be glory, majesty, dominion, and authority, before all time and now and forever. Amen. (Jude 1:24–25)

Dear friends, if our hearts do not condemn us, we have confidence before God and receive from him anything we ask, because we keep his commands and do what pleases him. And this is his command: to believe in the name of his Son, Jesus Christ, and to love one another as he commanded us. The one who keeps God's commands lives in him, and he in them. **And this is how we know that he lives in us: We know it by the Spirit he gave us**. 1 John 3:21-24

We exhorted each one of you and encouraged you and charged you to walk in a manner worthy of God, *who calls you* into his own kingdom and glory. (1 Thess. 2:12)

For you are a people holy to the Lord your God. *The Lord your God <u>has chosen you</u> to be a people for his treasured possession,* out of all the peoples who are on the face of the earth. It was not because you were more in number than any other people that the Lord set his love on you and chose you, for you were the fewest of all peoples, but it is because the Lord loves you and is keeping the oath that he swore to your fathers, that the Lord has brought you out with a mighty hand and redeemed you from the house of slavery, from the hand of Pharaoh king of Egypt. (Deut. 7:6–8)

Do not say in your heart, after the Lord your God has thrust them out before you, "It is because of my righteousness that the Lord has brought me in to possess this land," whereas it is because of the wickedness of these nations that the Lord is driving them out before you. <u>Not because of your righteousness or the uprightness of your heart are you going in to possess their land, but because of the wickedness of these nations the Lord your God is driving them out from before you, and that he may confirm the word that the</u>

<u>Lord swore to your fathers, to Abraham, to Isaac, and to Jacob</u>. Know, therefore, that the Lord your God is not giving you this good land to possess because of your righteousness, for you are a stubborn people. (Deut. 9:4–6)

And the LORD your God will circumcise your heart and the heart of your offspring, so that you will love the LORD your God with all your heart and with all your soul, that you may live. (Deuteronomy 30:6)

[Another great verse for the hat rack to trust God to save future family! I pray now for my granddaughters, and for their future husbands, and for their kids, as God has purposed, that God would save all of them for His name's sake and glory, for an eternity planned that is now being revealed over time.]

I will put My Spirit within you and cause you to walk in My statutes, and you will be careful to observe My ordinances. (Ezek. 36:27)

<u>I will make with them an everlasting covenant</u>, that <u>I will not turn away from doing good to them</u>. And <u>I will put the fear of me in their hearts</u>, that they may not turn from me. (Jeremiah 32:40)

I am God, and there is none like me, declaring the end from the beginning and from ancient times things not yet done, saying, "My counsel shall stand, and I will accomplish all my purpose." (Isa. 46:9–10)

Ascribe to the LORD Glory

A PSALM OF DAVID.

Ascribe to the LORD, O heavenly beings, ascribe to the LORD glory and strength. Ascribe to the LORD the glory due his name; worship the LORD in the splendor of holiness. The voice of the LORD is over the waters; the God of glory thunders, the LORD, over many waters. The voice of the LORD is powerful; the voice of the LORD is full of majesty. The voice of the LORD breaks the cedars; the LORD breaks the cedars of Lebanon. He makes Lebanon to skip like a calf, and Sirion like a young wild ox. The voice of the LORD flashes forth flames of fire. The voice of the LORD shakes the wilderness; the LORD shakes the wilderness of Kadesh. The voice of the LORD makes the deer give birth and strips the forests bare, *and in his temple all cry, "Glory!" The LORD sits enthroned over the flood; the LORD sits enthroned as king forever. May the LORD give strength to his people! May the LORD bless his people with peace!* (Ps. 29)

You have fixed all the boundaries of the earth; you have made summer and winter. (Ps. 74:17)

The Lord of hosts has sworn: "As I have planned, so shall it be, and as I have purposed, so shall it stand." (Isa. 14:24)

Therefore, my beloved, as you have always obeyed, so now, not only as in my presence but much more in my absence, **work out your own salvation with fear and trembling, for it is God**

who works in you, both to will and to work for his good pleasure. (Philippians 2:12–13)

Then Job arose and tore his robe and shaved his head and fell on the ground and worshiped. And he said, "Naked I came from my mother's womb, and naked shall I return. The LORD gave, and the LORD has taken away; **blessed be the name of the LORD**." In all this Job did not sin or charge God with wrong. (Job 1:20–22)

But he said to her, "You speak as one of the foolish women would speak. Shall we receive good from God, and shall we not receive evil?" In all this Job did not sin with his lips. (Job 2:10)

Our God is in the heavens; he does all that he pleases. (Psalms 115:3 ESV)

"For I have no pleasure in the death of anyone, declares the Lord GOD; so turn, and live." (Ezekiel 18:32)

Let no corrupting talk come out of your mouths, but only such as is good for building up, as fits the occasion, that it may give grace to those who hear. **And do not grieve the Holy Spirit of God**, *by whom you were sealed for the day of redemption.* Let all bitterness and wrath and anger and clamor and slander be put away from you, along with all malice. Be kind to one another, tenderhearted, forgiving one another, as God in Christ forgave you. (Ephesians 4:29–32)

And after you have suffered a little while, the God of all grace, **who has called you to his eternal**

glory in Christ, will himself restore, confirm, strengthen, and establish you. (1 Peter 5:10)

And Moses summoned all Israel and said to them: "You have seen all that the LORD did before your eyes in the land of Egypt, to Pharaoh and to all his servants and to all his land, the great trials that your eyes saw, the signs, and those great wonders. But to this day the LORD has not given you a heart to understand or eyes to see or ears to hear. (Deuteronomy 29:2–4)

Abimelech ruled over Israel three years. And God sent an evil spirit between Abimelech and the leaders of Shechem, and the leaders of Shechem dealt treacherously with Abimelech, that the violence done to the seventy sons of Jerubbaal might come, and their blood be laid on Abimelech their brother, who killed them, and on the men of Shechem, who strengthened his hands to kill his brothers. (Judges 9:22–24)

Compare Luke 22:3,

And Satan entered into Judas who was called Iscariot, belonging to the number of the twelve.

With Acts 2:23,

This Man, delivered over **by the predetermined plan and foreknowledge of God,** you nailed to a cross by the hands of godless men and put Him to death.

[See section on foreknowledge to understand this: it is not God seeing all future time but God calling out His will in the fullness of time.]

Compare 2 Corinthians 4:4,

> In whose case the god of this world has blinded the minds of the unbelieving so that they might not see the light of the gospel of the glory of Christ, who is the image of God.

With Romans 11:8–10,

> Just as it is written, "God gave them a spirit of stupor, Eyes to see not and ears to hear not, Down to this very day." And David says, "Let their table become a snare and a trap, And a stumbling block and a retribution to them. Let their eyes be darkened to see not, And bend their backs forever."

Compare 1 Chronicles 21:1,

> Then Satan stood up against Israel and moved David to number Israel.

With 2 Samuel 24:10,

> Now David's heart troubled him after he had numbered the people. So David said to the Lord, "I have sinned greatly in what I have done. But now, O Lord, please take away the iniquity of Your servant, for I have acted very foolishly."

> All the inhabitants of the earth are accounted as nothing, and he does according to his will among the host of heaven and among the inhabitants of

the earth; and none can stay his hand or say to him, "What have you done?" (Daniel 4:35 ESV)

Our God is in the heavens; he does all that he pleases. (Psalms 115:3 ESV)

We know that everyone who has been born of God does not keep on sinning, but he who was born of God protects him, and the evil one does not touch him. We know that we are from God, and the whole world lies in the power of the evil one. And we know that **the Son of God has come and has given us understanding**, so that we may know him who is true; and we are in him who is true, in his Son Jesus Christ. He is the true God and eternal life. (1 John 5:18–20)

Everyone who believes that Jesus is the Christ [=] is born of God, and everyone who loves the father [=] loves his child as well (1 John 5:1).

[John writes this like a math statement. If A = B, then B = A. Focusing on the first part of the verse, notice though that there is a condition to the *everyone*. Everyone is not equal to ALL people, for he adds the condition "who believes." Thus "everyone who believes" = (shows who are) "born of God."]

Flipping the subject line of the sentence to be shown more clearly as his object and the object as being the subject, for which it was as John has written, should make it easier to see that order is the same:

Born of God = everyone who believes that Jesus is the Christ.

Everyone who believes that Jesus is the Christ [A] = is born of God [B].

Thus, born of God [B] = everyone who believes [A].

A = B is equivalent to B=A.

Now the same can be said of 1 John 5:1b that everyone who loves Jesus [A] = loves the Father [B], but this equation is dependent upon the condition of 1 John 5:1a (who believes that Jesus is the Christ).

> We know that anyone born of God does not continue to sin; the One who was born of God keeps them safe, and the evil one cannot harm them. (1 John 5:18)

> We know also that the Son of God has come and has given us understanding, so that we may know him who is true. And we are in him who is true by being in his Son Jesus Christ. He is the true God and eternal life. (1 John 5:20)

> Humble yourselves, therefore, under the mighty hand of God so that at the proper time he may exalt you, casting all your anxieties on him, because he cares for you. Be sober-minded; be watchful. Your adversary the devil prowls around like a roaring lion, seeking someone to devour. Resist him, firm in your faith, knowing that the same kinds of suffering are being experienced by your brotherhood throughout the world. And after you have suffered a little while, the God of all grace, who has called you to his eternal glory in Christ, will himself restore, confirm, strengthen, and establish you. To him be the dominion forever and ever. Amen. (1 Pet. 5:6–11)

The Last Days

> Now concerning the coming of our Lord Jesus Christ and our being gathered together to him, we ask you, brothers, not to be quickly shaken in

mind or alarmed, either by a spirit or a spoken word, or a letter seeming to be from us, to the effect that the day of the Lord has come. Let no one deceive you in any way. For that day will not come, unless the rebellion comes first, and the man of lawlessness is revealed, the son of destruction, who opposes and exalts himself against every so-called god or object of worship, so that he takes his seat in the temple of God, proclaiming himself to be God. Do you not remember that when I was still with you I told you these things? And you know what is restraining him now so that he may be revealed in his time. For the mystery of lawlessness is already at work. Only he who now restrains it will do so until he is out of the way. And then the lawless one will be revealed, whom the Lord Jesus will kill with the breath of his mouth and bring to nothing by the appearance of his coming. The coming of the lawless one is by the activity of Satan with all power and false signs and wonders, and with all wicked deception for those who are perishing, because they refused to love the truth and so be saved. **Therefore God sends them a strong delusion, so that they may believe what is false, in order that all may be condemned who did not believe the truth but had pleasure in unrighteousness.** But we ought always to give thanks to God for you, brothers beloved by the Lord, **because God chose you as the firstfruits to be saved, through sanctification by the Spirit and belief in the truth.** To this he called you through our gospel, so that you may obtain the glory of our Lord Jesus Christ. (2 Thess. 2:1–14)

For my name's sake I defer my anger; **for the sake of my praise I restrain it for you,** that I may not cut you off. Behold, **I have refined you,** but not as silver; I have tried you in the furnace of affliction. **For my own sake, for my own sake, I do it,** for how should my name be profaned? **My glory I will not give to another.** (Isa. 48:9–11)

[Praise God for his name and for His glory!]

Like the appearance of the bow that is in the cloud on the day of rain, so was the appearance of the brightness all around. **Such was the appearance of the likeness of the glory of the LORD.** And when I saw it, I fell on my face, and I heard the voice of one speaking. (Ezek. 1:28)

Father, I desire that they also, whom you have given me, may be with me where I am, to see my glory that you have given me because you loved me before the foundation of the world. (John 17:24)

To the only wise God be glory forevermore through Jesus Christ! Amen. (Rom. 16:27)

That the God of our Lord Jesus Christ, the Father of glory, may give you the Spirit of wisdom and of revelation in the knowledge of him, having the eyes of your hearts enlightened, that you may know what is the hope to which he has called you, what are the riches of his glorious inheritance in the saints. (Eph. 1:17–18)

At the name of Jesus, every knee will bow...and every tongue confess that Jesus Christ is Lord, to the glory of God the Father. (Phil. 2:10–11)

For we are the circumcision, who worship by the Spirit of God and glory in Christ Jesus and put no confidence in the flesh. (Phil. 3:3)

1

God Messes with "Our Hearts"

Because man is inherently sinful,

> Therefore, just as sin came into the world through one man, and death through sin, and so death spread to all men because all sinned. (Rom. 5:12)

> For all have sinned and fall short of the glory of God. (Rom. 3:23)

And that no man seeks after God or righteousness:

> As it is written, "There is none righteous, not even one; There is none who understands, There is none who seeks for God; All have turned aside, together they have become useless; There is none who does good." (Rom. 3:10–12)

> For to set the mind on the flesh is death, but to set the mind on the Spirit is life and peace. For the mind that is set on the flesh is hostile to God, for it does not submit to God's law; indeed, it cannot. Those who are in the flesh cannot please God. (Rom. 8:6–8)

A lot of late twentieth and early twenty-first century Western Protestant-based church doctrines—at least those that I have been exposed to—have taken liberties to say that man's will is free and unencumbered to decide and that God has "gifted" man to be the initiator of believing in Jesus. That God counts on or even draws all people to make a good choice to believe from within their own will.

Many of those church doctrines would ascribe to also say that God does initiate a process for all men to believe; however, they lean heavily into man's perspective of "deciding" to accept Jesus for the "last mile," thus preserving the choice of man as being a "better believer," and a term many use, not as a "robot," which would take away from man "sincerely" loving God—from their self-determination will.

My further understanding of this free-will form of doctrine claims that God doesn't "interfere" with man's will to the point of "making" someone believe, for God really wants those who truly want to choose Him and not those for whom God does the choosing, for wouldn't that make more sense? Then once they choose to believe or accept Jesus, then God makes them born again and thus even secures them as one of His sheep.

I want to be tender to express my love to those who say that, that they made the first deciding decision to believe in Jesus as Lord and Savior, which from the <u>self-perspective</u> of the moment, I would agree that's what happened in their eyes. The Gospel was preached, they heard it, and they prayed to ask "Jesus to come into their heart" and they believed. Amen!

However, from God's perspective, remembering that God's view is the best view, He declares it is His work of changing hearts, His work of saving, and His work of keeping.

> Behold, the days are coming, declares the Lord, when <u>I will make</u> a new covenant with the house of Israel and the house of Judah, not like the covenant that I made with their fathers on the day when I took them by the hand to bring them out of the land of Egypt, my covenant that they

broke, though I was their husband, declares the Lord. For this is the covenant that I will make with the house of Israel after those days, declares the Lord: I will put my law within them, and I will write it on their hearts. And I will be their God, and they shall be my people. (Jer. 31:31–33)

And I will give you a new heart, and a new spirit I will put within you. And I will remove the heart of stone from your flesh and give you a heart of flesh. And **I will put my Spirit within you and cause you to walk in my statutes and be careful to obey my rules**. (Ezek. 36:26–27)

The LORD your God will circumcise your heart and the heart of your offspring, so that you will love the LORD your God with all your heart and with all your soul, that you may live. (Deut. 30:6)

But it is not as though the word of God has failed. For not all who are descended from Israel belong to Israel, and not all are children of Abraham because they are his offspring, but "Through Isaac shall your offspring be named." This means that it is not the children of the flesh who are the children of God, but the children of the promise are counted as offspring. (Rom. 9:6–8)

Therefore he [Jesus] is the mediator of a new covenant, so that those who are called may receive the promised eternal inheritance, since a death has occurred that redeems them from the transgressions committed under the first covenant. (Heb. 9:15)

> And he took bread, and when he had given thanks, he broke it and gave it to them, saying, "This is my body, which is given for you. Do this in remembrance of me." And likewise the cup after they had eaten, saying, "This cup that is poured out for you is the new covenant in my blood." (Luke 22:19–20)

All of us are born sinners, blinded to the glory of the Gospel of Christ. As sinners, we make and even enjoy our choices of living in and for sin, for our will is and now was under the control of sin and influenced by Satan.

> And you were dead in the trespasses and sins in which you once walked, following the course of this world, following the prince of the power of the air, the spirit that is now at work in the sons of disobedience—among whom we all once lived in the passions of our flesh, carrying out the desires of the body and the mind, and were by nature children of wrath, like the rest of mankind. BUT GOD, being rich in mercy, because of the great love with which he loved us, even when we were dead in our trespasses, made us alive together with Christ—by grace you have been saved—and raised us up with him and seated us with him in the heavenly places in Christ Jesus, so that in the coming ages he might show the immeasurable riches of his grace in kindness toward us in Christ Jesus. For by grace you have been saved through faith. And this is not your own doing; it is the gift of God, not a result of works, so that no one may boast. For we are his workmanship, created in Christ Jesus for good works, which God prepared beforehand, that we should walk in them. (Eph. 2:1–10)

In their case **the god of this world has blinded the minds of the unbelievers, to keep them from seeing the light of the gospel of the glory of Christ, who is the image of God**. For what we proclaim is not ourselves, but Jesus Christ as Lord, with ourselves as your servants for Jesus' sake. For <u>God</u>, who said, "Let light shine out of darkness," **<u>has shone</u> in our hearts to give the light of the knowledge of the glory of God in the face of Jesus Christ**. (2 Cor. 4:4–6)

"The Building Is on Fire" Analogy

All analogies from a human perspective have points of contention, and so does this one, but if you look to the core point, I trust it can help you understand how salvation directed by God and believing by man works together.

Let us say you live in a large apartment building, say with one thousand apartments. Let us also say that you and everyone in the building are sound sleepers. Real sound sleepers!

One night, all were asleep in their beds, and a big fire breaks out, and the one-thousand-unit apartment is engulfed in flames. As sound sleepers, all folks are sleeping within their apartments and are oblivious to the fire around them. Even with the fire alarm blaring, and yet as sound sleepers, no one heard the alarm.

The fire was so big and enraged that the fire company saw the fire from a distance and came quickly to the scene.

The fireman, wearing his protective gear, entered the building, and the fireman was knocking on your door amongst the flames around you. You, being a sound sleeper, did not hear the knock, for being asleep, you are not aware of the danger around you.

The flames are huge, the fireman is persistent, he breaks down the door, you are still asleep, and the danger continues. He yells to you, "Fire, get up and come with me," but you are still asleep, as all others within the building.

He then comes over to your bed and shakes you; you now are awakened; and you see the fireman, the flames, and the smoke all around, and the fireman says, "Let me take you out from here."

Your eyes now being opened, you now see the danger, you now see the path to safety…what do you do?

You "choose" to let the fireman save you.

So to help having message sent = message received, the building represents living life. The fire represents sin. Being a sound sleeper represents living in sin. The fire alarm represents the prophets and the Bible. The fire response loosely represents God the Father, God the Son, God the Holy Spirit, whereas the firehouse—God the Father— sends the fireman; the fireman represents Jesus, who does the work of saving and putting out the fire (yes, I know this part is weak in that the fireman doesn't save through dying and resurrecting for our sins in this story—just focus on His going and saving); and the shaking of you to awaken you represents the Holy Spirit (which is the focal point of my analogy).

Again, do not go too far beyond the definitions, for the intent is to show that being saved is God's initiation, God's actions, and God's awakening and not man by his free will. For once awakened, the choice to being saved from the fire when the fire is real and emi-nent would be 100 percent. For now being awakened in seeing and knowing the danger, who would refuse?

Your will of choice. Was it free? It was within sin and blinded to the light of the Gospel of Christ. Let us go back to 2 Corinthians 4:4–6:

> In their case the god of this world has blinded the minds of the unbelievers, to keep them from see-ing the light of the gospel of the glory of Christ, who is the image of God. For what we proclaim is not ourselves, but Jesus Christ as Lord, with ourselves as your servants for Jesus' sake. For God, who said, "Let light shine out of darkness," has shone in our hearts to give the light of the

knowledge of the glory of God in the face of Jesus Christ.

So...to the events of the fire, can you now see being awakened first in order for you to see the danger and then the escape route to be saved is via the fireman? Thus, being first born again to believe is how God works within our hearts and not believing first then being born again?

> Do not marvel that I said to you, "You must be born again." (John 3:7)

Lidia in Acts 16:14–15, knew God and even worshipped him, and yet Luke writes that it was on that day that Paul was in the city that the Lord opened her heart to the Gospel Paul preached and believed and was baptized.

> And a certain woman named Lydia, a seller of purple, of the city of Thyatira, one that worshipped God, heard us: whose heart the Lord opened to give heed unto the things which were spoken by Paul. And after she was baptized, and her household as well.

And I have been using the word *decision* on purpose. We make decisions. That is what we do in life. I decide what time to wake up by setting an alarm. What I eat or do not eat for breakfast or what to do each day. And within the sphere of my surroundings, there could be thousands of people around me making their own decisions today, thus a great opportunity to change an earlier decision of the left turn instead of a right.

But here in the context of deciding or accepting Jesus as your Savior...deciding means believing.

> But to all who did **receive him, [parenthetically defined as all] who believed in his name,** he

gave the right to become children of God, <u>who were born, not of blood nor of the will of the flesh nor of the will of man, but of God.</u> (John 1:12–13)

This is the working of the Holy Spirit, awakening you and me to the Gospel of Christ prior to "deciding-accepting-believing," thus being born again, first, in order to receive-believe-accept Christ that God has shown the glory of Christ within our hearts.

For God, who said, "Let light shine out of darkness," has shone in our hearts to give the light of the knowledge of the glory of God in the face of Jesus Christ. (2 Cor. 4:4)

Jesus tells Nicodemus in John 3:3, "Truly, truly, I say to you, unless one is born again he cannot see the kingdom of God."

Receiving (or accepting or believing) Jesus does not then make us born again, then salvation would be because of our efforts. You must be born again, first, to see the wisdom and the glory of God in salvation. Your and my salvation is all of God's work, even the work of receiving-accepting-believing.

The fireman shaking you to awaken you, my hearing the Gospel again the second year of church camp, and the Holy Spirit shining the light of the glory of Jesus within our heart is the necessary first step of many steps happening that God works within our hearts at the time of our realizing and seeing the glory of God and the wisdom of God in His calling us to faith.

Let us take a moment to look at the Jailer of Paul and Silas in Acts 16:

So, setting sail from Troas, we made a direct voyage to Samothrace, and the following day to Neapolis, and from there to Philippi, which is a leading city of the district of Macedonia and a Roman colony. We remained in this city some days. As we were going to the place of prayer, we were met by a slave girl who had a spirit of divination and brought her owners much gain by fortune-telling. She followed Paul and us, crying out, "These men are servants of the Most High God, who proclaim to you the way of salvation." And this she kept doing for many days. Paul, having become greatly annoyed, turned, and said to the spirit, "I command you in the name of Jesus Christ to come out of her." And it came out that very hour. But when her owners saw that their hope of gain was gone, they seized Paul and Silas and dragged them into the marketplace before the rulers. And when they had brought them to the magistrates, they said, "These men are Jews, and they are disturbing our city. They advocate customs that are not lawful for us as Romans to accept or practice." The crowd joined in attacking them, and the magistrates tore the garments off them and gave orders to beat them with rods. And when they had inflicted many blows upon them, they threw them into prison, ordering the jailer to keep them safely. Having received this order, he put them into the inner prison and fastened their feet in the stocks. About midnight Paul and Silas were praying and singing hymns to God, and the prisoners were listening to them, and suddenly there was a great earthquake, so that the foundations of the prison were shaken. And immediately all the doors were opened, and everyone's bonds were unfastened. When the jailer woke and saw that the prison doors were open, he drew his sword and was about to kill himself, supposing that the prisoners had escaped. But Paul cried with a loud voice, "Do not harm yourself, for we are all here." And the jailer called for lights and rushed in, and trembling with fear he fell down before Paul and Silas. Then he brought them out and said, **"Sirs, what must I do to be saved?" And they said, "Believe in the Lord Jesus**, and you will be saved, you and your household." And they spoke the word of the Lord to him and to all who were in his house. And he took them the same hour of the night and washed their wounds; and he was baptized at once, he and all his family. Then he brought them up into his house and set food before them. And he rejoiced along with his entire household that he had believed in God. (Acts 16:11–34)

The owners of a demon-possessed slave girl got revenge on Paul when he cast out the demon from this girl and thus took away their way of making fast money. They had the magistrates rule against Paul and Silas; they then had them beaten and locked away in prison.

But look at what God did: He saved the jailer and his family.

The jailer asks Paul, "What must I do to be saved?" For here in his heart and mind, he has come to the view, and, may I add, a divinely created view, that he needs what Paul has. This is not as much a choice but an action of faith…a God-given faith that is congruent with the action of our will.

So my question about deciding about Jesus? If left only to our will to decide, is then the decision stable? For revisiting Romans 3, there is none who understands, there is none who seeks, and there is none who does good.

John Piper clarifies it best for me when he writes,

"Free will" is a name put on a mystery. But it is not the biblical name. Because the Bible never teaches that there is such a thing as ultimate human, or ultimate demonic, self-determination. That is a philosophical notion forced onto the Bible, not taught by the Bible. In fact, that philosophical notion was one of Satan's first designs for humanity—to persuade Adam and Eve that they could be ultimately self-determining, and that this would be good for them (Genesis 3:4–5). Both of those ideas were false. They could not become ultimately self-determining, and it was deadly for them to. The human race has been ruined by these notions ever since.[1]

I hear what some of you are thinking—well, not really—but I would have asked: well, does God work in all men's hearts?

In a word, YES.

> The heart of man plans his way, but the Lord establishes his steps. (Prov. 16:9)

Let us explore.

---

[1] John Piper, "How Did Evil Begin?"

2

Does God Then Work within the Hearts of All Men?

What a difficult question to ask. For man is accountable for the sin he does, and yet there are obvious times that the grace of God moves upon the unregenerate heart, to the counsel of the will of God. For a modern example, you might see a man who loves his family, gives to charities of time and monies, and does things that one would expect of someone who is a believer in Christ, but yet he doesn't see Jesus as his personal Savior from sin and the Lord of his life.

And everyone misquotes the saying "Why do bad things happen to 'good' people?" made popular by Harold Kushner. When really, no one is good. But no one ever asks, "Why do good things happen to bad people?" for which there is a biblical answer: God's mercy and temporal grace.

> You have heard that it was said, "You shall love your neighbor and hate your enemy." But I say to you, Love your enemies and pray for those who persecute you, so that you may be sons of your Father who is in heaven. **For he makes his sun rise on the evil and on the good, and sends rain on the just and on the unjust.** (Matt. 5:43–45)

So God brings the sun (good works, blessings in life) on all men, and He also brings rain (taking the opposite view from the sun—trials, bad things) on all men as well.

Let us look at a few examples of God working within hearts of nonbelievers within the Bible, and they stay nonbelievers.

Abraham and Abimelech

> From there Abraham journeyed toward the territory of the Negeb and lived between Kadesh and Shur; and he sojourned in Gerar. And Abraham said of Sarah his wife, "She is my sister." And Abimelech king of Gerar sent and took Sarah. But God came to Abimelech in a dream by night and said to him, "Behold, you are a dead man because of the woman whom you have taken, for she is a man's wife." Now Abimelech had not approached her. So he said, "Lord, will you kill an innocent people? Did he not himself say to me, 'She is my sister'? And she herself said, 'He is my brother.' In the integrity of my heart and the innocence of my hands I have done this." Then God said to him in the dream, "Yes, I know that you have done this in the integrity of your heart, and it was I who kept you from sinning against me. **Therefore I did not let you touch her**. Now then, return the man's wife, for he is a prophet, so that he will pray for you, and you shall live. But if you do not return her, know that you shall surely die, you and all who are yours." (Gen. 20:1–7)

King Abimelech had his eye on Sarah, Abraham's wife, and wanted her for his own. But God steps in, into the thoughts of Abimelech as a dream and told him, "You better not, for Sarah is Abraham's wife." And Abimelech even converses with God, and not his god but God Almighty, telling God that he stopped himself. And what was God's reply? "I did not let you touch her!" So God interjects into the actions of Abimelech and stops the action of his sin. There is a whole sermon on this alone, but let us now look at King Cyrus.

King Cyrus

Who says of Cyrus, "He is my shepherd, and he shall fulfill all my purpose"; saying of Jerusalem, "She shall be built," and of the temple, "Your foundation shall be laid."

Thus says the LORD to his anointed, to Cyrus, whose right hand I have grasped, to subdue nations before him and to loose the belts of kings, to open doors before him that gates may not be closed: "I will go before you and level the exalted places, I will break in pieces the doors of bronze and cut through the bars of iron, I will give you the treasures of darkness and the hoards in secret places, that you may know that it is I, the LORD, the God of Israel, who call you by your name. For the sake of my servant Jacob, and Israel my chosen, I call you by your name, I name you, though you do not know me. I am the LORD, and there is no other, besides me there is no God; I equip you, though you do not know me, that people may know, from the rising of the sun and from the west, that there is none besides me; I am the LORD, and there is no other. (Isa. 44:28–45:6)

Now in the first year of Cyrus king of Persia, that the word of the LORD by the mouth of Jeremiah might be fulfilled, the LORD stirred up the spirit of Cyrus king of Persia, so that he made a proclamation throughout all his kingdom and also put it in writing: "Thus says Cyrus king of Persia, 'The LORD, the God of heaven, has given me all the kingdoms of the earth, and he has charged me to build him a house at Jerusalem, which is in Judah. Whoever is among you of all his people, may the LORD his God be with him. Let him go up.'" (2 Chron. 36:22–23)

In the first year of Cyrus king of Persia, that the word of the LORD by the mouth of Jeremiah might be fulfilled, <u>the LORD stirred up the spirit of Cyrus king of Persia</u>, so that he made a proclamation throughout all his kingdom and also put it in writing:

    "Thus says Cyrus king of Persia: **The LORD, the God of heaven, has given me all the kingdoms of the earth, and he has charged me to build him a house at Jerusalem, which is in Judah.** Whoever is among you of all his people, may his God be with him, and let him go up to Jerusalem, which is in Judah, and rebuild the house of the LORD, the God of Israel—he is the God who is in Jerusalem. And let each survivor, in whatever place he sojourns, be assisted by the men of his place with silver and gold, with goods and with beasts, besides freewill offerings for the house of God that is in Jerusalem." (Ezra 1:1–4)

What is also amazing is that Isaiah lived and was a prophet to Israel about 150 years before Cyrus was born and came to rule. So God gave Isaiah not only the prophesy of rebuilding the temple but also the name of the king yet to be born! And also note that King Cyrus gives God the credit for stirring him up to allow Ezra to go back and rebuild the temple, AND King Cyrus gave him the money to do it!

And the story even gets better. Not only did God move upon King Cyrus to send Ezra back to Jerusalem to rebuild the temple but to also provide the finances to do so. AND THEN, God also moved upon the hearts of a remnant of Israel to stir within them to go back to do the work:

> Then rose up the heads of the fathers' houses of Judah and Benjamin, and the priests and the Levites, everyone whose spirit <u>God had stirred to go up to rebuild the house of the LORD that is in Jerusalem</u>. (Ezra 1:5)

And another reference is from Jesus Himself, to Pontius Pilate while Jesus was in Pilate's court.

Pontius Pilate

> Then Pilate took Jesus and flogged him. And the soldiers twisted together a crown of thorns and put it on his head and arrayed him in a purple robe. They came up to him, saying, "Hail, King of the Jews!" and struck him with their hands. Pilate went out again and said to them, "See, I am bringing him out to you that you may know that I find no guilt in him." So Jesus came out, wearing the crown of thorns and the purple robe. Pilate said to them, "Behold the man!" When the chief priests and the officers saw him, they cried out, "Crucify him, crucify him!" Pilate said to them, "Take him yourselves and crucify him, for I find no guilt in him." The Jews answered him, "We have a law, and according to that law he ought to die because he has made himself the Son of God." When Pilate heard this statement, he was even more afraid. He entered his headquarters again and said to Jesus, "Where are you

from?" But Jesus gave him no answer. So Pilate said to him, "You will not speak to me? **Do you not know that I have authority to release you and authority to crucify you?" Jesus answered him, "You would have no authority over me at all unless it had been given you from above. Therefore he who delivered me over to you has the greater sin."** (John 19:1–11)

And Then There Is Pharaoh

The first three biblical references show God interacting with nonbelievers who have some respect for God. Abimelech and King Cyrus knew it was God that they were dealing with, the God of Abraham and Isaac and Jacob. But Pharaoh, he was a rascal. And obstinate. And downright nasty against Israel.

> And the LORD said to Moses, "When you go back to Egypt, see that you do before Pharaoh all the miracles <u>that I have put in your power. But I will harden his heart, so that he will not let the people go</u>." (Exod. 4:21)

> And the LORD said to Moses, "See, I have made you like God to Pharaoh, and your brother Aaron shall be your prophet. You shall speak all that I command you, and your brother Aaron shall tell Pharaoh to let the people of Israel go out of his land. **But I will harden Pharaoh's heart, and though I multiply my signs and wonders in the land of Egypt, Pharaoh will not listen to you. Then I will lay my hand on Egypt and bring my hosts, my people the children of Israel, out of the land of Egypt by great acts of judgment.** The Egyptians shall know that I am the LORD, when I stretch out my hand against Egypt and

bring out the people of Israel from among them."
(Exod. 7:1–5)

Then the LORD said to Moses, "Tell the people of Israel to turn back and encamp in front
of Pi-hahiroth, between Migdol and the sea, in
front of Baal-zephon; you shall encamp facing it,
by the sea. For Pharaoh will say of the people
of Israel, 'They are wandering in the land; the
wilderness has shut them in.' **And I will harden
Pharaoh's heart, and he will pursue them, and
I will get glory over Pharaoh and all his host,
and the Egyptians shall know that I am the
LORD.**" And they did so. (Exod. 14:1–4)

And a bonus scenario.

God Gives Words and Wisdom to a Donkey!

And God came to Balaam at night and said to
him, "If the men have come to call you, rise,
go with them; but only do what I tell you." So
Balaam rose in the morning and saddled his
donkey and went with the princes of Moab. But
God's anger was kindled because he went, and
the angel of the LORD took his stand in the way
as his adversary. Now he was riding on the donkey, and his two servants were with him. And the
donkey saw the angel of the LORD standing in
the road, with a drawn sword in his hand. And
the donkey turned aside out of the road and went
into the field. And Balaam struck the donkey, to
turn her into the road. Then the angel of the
LORD stood in a narrow path between the vine-
yards, with a wall on either side. And when the
donkey saw the angel of the LORD, she pushed

against the wall and pressed Balaam's foot against the wall. So he struck her again. Then the angel of the LORD went ahead and stood in a narrow place, where there was no way to turn either to the right or to the left. When the donkey saw the angel of the LORD, she lay down under Balaam. And Balaam's anger was kindled, and he struck the donkey with his staff. <u>Then the LORD opened the mouth of the donkey, and she said to Balaam, "What have I done to you, that you have struck me these three times?"</u> And Balaam said to the donkey, "Because you have made a fool of me. I wish I had a sword in my hand, for then I would kill you." And the donkey said to Balaam, "Am I not your donkey, on which you have ridden all your life long to this day? Is it my habit to treat you this way?" And he said, "No." *Then the LORD opened the eyes of Balaam,* and he saw the angel of the LORD standing in the way, with his drawn sword in his hand. And he bowed down and fell on his face. And the angel of the LORD said to him, "Why have you struck your donkey these three times? Behold, I have come out to oppose you because your way is perverse before me. The donkey saw me and turned aside before me these three times. If she had not turned aside from me, surely just now I would have killed you and let her live." Then Balaam said to the angel of the LORD, "I have sinned, for I did not know that you stood in the road against me. Now therefore, if it is evil in your sight, I will turn back." And the angel of the LORD said to Balaam, "Go with the men, but speak only the word that I tell you." So Balaam went on with the princes of Balak. (Num. 22:20–35)

Wow! So I trust that you and the Lord are having a great conversation right about now and you are in awe of His glory as I am. So the next step to examine is to look a bit deeper into the will of God in salvation and the desire of God that all men repent and be saved.

(Also take note of "the angel [messenger] of the Lord," which I believe is Jesus preincarnate, but leave that here for another time of study, Lord willing.)

Let us now consider…

3

The Mild Tension to Understand the Differences between God's Will and His Desires

It may be possible to hear an objection or two still stirring within some that God desires that all men repent and come to Him as being His will. Let us examine:

> This is good, and it is pleasing in the sight <u>of God our Savior, who desires all people to be saved and to come to the knowledge of the truth</u>. For there is one God, and there is one mediator between God and men, the man Christ Jesus, who gave himself as a ransom for all, which is the testimony given at the proper time. For this I was appointed a preacher and an apostle (I am telling the truth, I am not lying), a teacher of the Gentiles in faith and truth. (1 Tim. 2:3–7)

With...

> And the Lord's servant must not be quarrelsome but kind to everyone, able to teach, patiently enduring evil, correcting his opponents with gentleness. <u>God may perhaps grant them repentance</u>

leading to a knowledge of the truth, and they
may come to their senses and escape from the
snare of the devil, after being captured by him to
do his will. (2 Tim. 2: 24–26)

In 1 Timothy 2:4, Paul tells Timothy that God desires all people to be saved and come to the knowledge of the truth, and yet he further tells Timothy in 2 Timothy that it is God who grants "them" repentance leading to the knowledge of the truth.

Paul says on one hand God wants (desires) all people to be saved and for "their coming" to the knowledge of the truth, and yet on the other hand, he says that God may perhaps grant them—which are those in opposition to the Gospel message within the church Timothy is pastoring—repentance leading to faith.

It says in 1, Timothy 2:3–7 that God wants (desires) all people to take the action to come to Him.

Then 2 Timothy 2:24–26 says God takes the action to grant repentance, which is connected to understanding the knowledge of the truth of the gospel, which then results in them coming to their senses—i.e., the light of the Gospel now making sense (1 Cor. 4:4), and God gives them faith to believe.

But we know that through Romans 3, no man can come to God on their own accord, for their heart is selfish, so this must define that God's will and God's desires are not the same, unless God "causes" the motion of man to come to Him, and thus it is God's action of His will and not man's.

The same could be said regarding this:

The Lord is not slow to fulfill his promise as
some count slowness, but is patient toward you,
not wishing that any should perish, but that all
should reach repentance. (2 Pet. 3:9)

Whereas Peter is offering us a glimpse into the character of God and not so much God's will to save all people. And as with Paul, the invitation to repent is wide open. However, because of man's inherent desire for sin, no man wants to repent and seek after God on his own—thus the purpose of the new covenant.

Now again, those who love God and seek after Him will find Him

> I love those who love me, and those who seek me
> diligently find me. (Prov. 8:17)

But I see a potential contradiction, but there are no contradictions within scripture, so we need to also consider Romans 3:10–11:

> As it is written: "None is righteous, no, not one;
> no one understands; no one seeks for God."

Hmmm. See the potential tension: "Those who seek me diligently find Me." And "No one understands; no one seeks for God."

The sum of the word is truth (Ps. 119:160), so both statements are true, as is "God our Savior, who desires all people to be saved and come to the knowledge of the truth…who gave Himself a ransom for all." So is this a paradox within the word, or does this have a perfect fit into the will of God? And if so, how so?

We may first see Proverbs 8:17 as an open-ended statement of man seeking God; it is conditional. It is open for all, yet unless God's love is within their heart, the open call goes unanswered.

> And hope does not put us to shame, because
> God's love has been poured into our hearts
> through the Holy Spirit who has been given to
> us. (Rom. 5:5)

> We love because he first loved us. (1 John 4:19)

Another verse that declares more of God's character than His will or His desires is:

> Have I any pleasure in the death of the wicked, declares the Lord GOD, and not rather that he should turn from his way and live? (Ezek. 18:23)

As with the others, the invitation (proclamation) to repent is wide open, as is the GOSPEL of salvation. So in point, God's declarative will is different from His desires, for His desires put the work on man's doing, which man cannot do because of his sin and self-centeredness. Thus, God's will is His efforts for His glory, and His desires for man is God's lament for man to seek Him.

A potential question asks:

Doesn't God Put the Desire to Believe into All People?

The intent is to say that God gives everyone an equal chance to believe, and if someone does not believe in Jesus, then it is their fault, not God's "choice" for them. Tenderly as I can, this view does not have the scriptural support it needs to make that statement true.

The Gospel of salvation is a wide-open call, open to any and everyone. However, no one comes. No one comes on their own volition; no one overcomes their own blindness to sin.

It starts with the fall; and then through Abraham, Isaac, and Jacob; and travels through the new covenant and Jeremiah 31:31–33 and Ezekiel 36 through Romans 3, 9, and 10, into Hebrews and many other scriptural references I have provide within pre-chapter.

Humbly stated, salvation is of and for God, and He chose everything before He created anything. The stars in the sky, the number of galaxies and planets. The angels and realms in Heaven. The drops of water and grains of sand, to why the sun and the Earth and the Earth's tilt and the four seasons to the northern and southern hemisphere, to all the plants and animals, and to man and to their time and place. Man should know who God is as Paul declares within

THE SOVEREIGNTY OF GOD IN OUR DAILY LIVES

Romans 1, and yet all men are sinful and, to be blunt, enjoy it. God gave man the desire to find God, and man already messed it up.

> For the wrath of God is revealed from heaven against all ungodliness and unrighteousness of men, who by their unrighteousness suppress the truth. For what can be known about God is plain to them, because God has shown it to them. For his invisible attributes, namely, his eternal power and divine nature, have been clearly perceived, ever since the creation of the world, in the things that have been made. So they are without excuse. For although they knew God, they did not honor him as God or give thanks to him, but they became futile in their thinking, and their foolish hearts were darkened. Claiming to be wise, they became fools, and exchanged the glory of the immortal God for images resembling mortal man and birds and animals and creeping things. (Rom. 1:18–23)

All men are sinners, and no one is righteous, and none seeks for God. God, being holy and righteous, demands justice for sin, so as Ephesians declares, everyone deserves the punishment for sin! But God, who is rich in mercy, saves some. And as Paul asks rhetorically, in God's saving some, is He unfair?

> And not only so, but also when Rebekah had conceived children by one man, our forefather Isaac, though they were not yet born and had done nothing either good or bad—in order that God's purpose of election might continue, not because of works but because of him who calls—she was told, "The older will serve the younger." As it is written, "Jacob I loved, but Esau I hated." What shall we say then? Is there injustice on God's part?

By no means! For he says to Moses, "I will have mercy on whom I have mercy, and I will have compassion on whom I have compassion." So then it depends not on human will or exertion, but on God, who has mercy. For the Scripture says to Pharaoh, "For this very purpose I have raised you up, that I might show my power in you, and that my name might be proclaimed in all the earth." So then he has mercy on whomever he wills, and he hardens whomever he wills. You will say to me then, "Why does he still find fault? For who can resist his will?" But who are you, O man, to answer back to God? Will what is molded say to its molder, "Why have you made me like this?" Has the potter no right over the clay, to make out of the same lump one vessel for honorable use and another for dishonorable use? What if God, desiring to show his wrath and to make known his power, has endured with much patience vessels of wrath prepared for destruction, in order to make known the riches of his glory for vessels of mercy, which he has prepared beforehand for glory—even us whom he has called, not from the Jews only but also from the Gentiles? (Rom. 9:10–24)

Adding Another Dimension to the "Building Is on Fire" Analogy

Going back to Chapter 1 and the "The Building Is on Fire" analogy, of the one-thousand-unit apartment complex you live in, you will remember the story was given to showcase by a weak example how one needs to be "awakened" spiritually in order for them to "see their sinfulness and to see the light of the glory of Jesus." Now let us add another layer by supplying definition to the entire building's tenants of one thousand folks and the fireman saving some but not all that night.

You come to learn soon after being rescued that the fireman only saved three hundred people that night. And it was not a matter of his ability that three hundred were saved; it is what he did that is in focus. A television news crew arrived shortly after your rescue, and they asked you about your experience.

You testify that you were awakened by the fireman and then saw the danger, and he then saved you from the fire. You then give the fireman great credit for saving you from the danger and perils of being trapped in the raging fire.

The news reporter then answers back and stated, "How lucky you were, for you were one of three hundred people saved that night, for over seven hundred others perished." Your heart sinks, for now knowing that seven hundred people died through not surviving the fire, so you sit down on the curb and ask yourself, why me?

Some thoughts you now might be having:

- Are you now angry with the fireman for not saving all one thousand people?
- Or are you now questioning the skills of the fireman for not doing his job better, for he only saved 30 percent of the tenants?
- Or are you mad at the building owner for not building the building with a better fire prevention plan?
- Or again why me and not the next-door neighbor?
- Or do you just remain thankful that the fireman knocked down your door, he awakened you to see the peril, and then he saved you from danger and imminent death?

Now thinking to yourself that the fireman had the time to save more people, or that he could have called for more resources, you are now placing yourself into the fireman's role, for when you were not even awake to be saved in the first place, for you now are thinking that the fireman could have done a better job.

For you see, sin is awful, and in your salvation—being now saved by the fireman when you were blinded to the truth of the building is on fire—you could fall into joining the crowd and critique the fireman.

The news media quickly looks for another angle to cover, that of the ones who were not saved. Is the fireman now a bad fireman for only saving three hundred people? Of course not! He saved all three hundred people to the doors he broke down and the rooms he entered. By rights, all one thousand would have died that night if it were not for the fire response team, so let the news report show that salvation came that night to three hundred folks rescued from the building on fire and that the fireman deserves all the credit for saving them from the sin of fire. To those seven hundred who died, if they only could hear the alarm, smell the smoke, and hear the cry of "FIRE, run to safety!" The story tonight is not about the seven hundred, but about the one thousand people trapped unawares and three hundred were saved!

By application, this section is not about the news reporter doing her job; it is not even about you and the other 299 people or even the other seven hundred folks. It is about critiquing the fireman doing his job.

In like fashion, we all are sinners within our own building-on-fire-of-life analogy. And all of us will die because of sin. BUT GOD, who is rich in mercy and grace, provides an avenue of escape that is through Jesus Christ, His Son. But nobody hears the alarm…the prophets, the Bible, and the preachers. Everyone is sound asleep enjoying their sin. So to the fireman, now breaking down our doors and shaking us—which is as the Holy Spirit awakening us (and changing our hearts)—to us now seeing the danger, the sin, the Savior before us, now we are awakened; we jump into the arms of the fireman, and he carries us to safety! And in the process of being saved, you see that this as a one-on-one event, for your sin is all around you and is consuming you, and death is at your door, so you have no time to get your valuables (church membership, good deeds outweighing the bad deeds, being a good person, etc.), nor are you thinking that those valuables are important now. You see life and freedom and a Savior right at your bed post, and you move!

For in this story, the fire will consume this building and everything within! The alarm is loudly ringing, but folks are still sleeping in sin, enjoying the life they went to bed with, oblivious to the alarms of life around them. But the fireman came to this building tonight, he knocked down the doors that he knocked down, and salvation came to three hundred folks this night. Again, I ask, is the fireman wrong to save three hundred folks today?

And tomorrow, he goes to another building on fire, and the next day and the next day—for he goes out and saves more, is he wrong to save whom he saves? Everyone within each building is destined to die unless the fireman breaks the door and snatches them from the death of the blaze. Oh, by the way, as a sound sleeper, there was nothing you or the other 299 that night did or could do for the fireman to "pick" you and your apartment. It was all the fireman's call as to why you.

For me this helps me see how humbling this is. That God saved me from my wages of being a sinner. That He chose me to pour out His grace upon me and to put down the fire and quench the sin of my life for His glory and my eternal benefit makes me willingly and gratefully bow down and worship my Savior, my Lord, and my King.

So what do we do now? We thank the Lord for His saving us, and we turn from the sin we once were oblivious to, and we continually worship and work for Him. So now we have a testimony of God's grace and mercy. We now have a personal relationship with Jesus. We now have a mission to share the good news of Jesus Christ. For you see, this analogy has one and now two points of focus and fails in other areas if we wander from the focus.

The first story is about God awakening our hearts. The second additive story is to show that God saves those He saves. Is God unfair for not saving all? Do not all people have the alarm blaring to warn them and act?

But now there is more! There is life after being saved from the fire. The hope and promise of eternal life! So now you and I become part of the fire team. We go out to as many as would hear and share the good news of Jesus Christ! Being ambassadors for the fireman! We become the fire alarms in the analogy.

Pray and testify to the lost members of our family, our community, our workplace, and the world, telling them that their building is on fire and for their need of Jesus, their Savior. That Jesus came to save them, and trust that God will take our testimony of the Gospel of Christ and shake them to awaken their hearts to respond! And pray that God will get the glory for His saving others!

This is…

Why Prayer Is So Important!

This is one of the strongest reasons to pray for the lost, within our family, within our neighborhood, within our workplaces, and within our churches. For God changes hearts unto salvation. And at times, God will place a call within us to pray for someone's salvation. And in those times, God saves them, and we all get to see the glory of Christ in saving them! It is not to say that those we do not pray for will not be saved. But what I am saying is I have been awakened from various hours of sleep to pray for folks, and I have seen God's answering those prayers to the glory of His grace!

Let us now circle back to

Ransom for All vs. for the Many

This is good, and it is pleasing in the sight of God our Savior, who desires all people to be saved and to come to the knowledge of the truth. For there is one God, and there is one mediator between God and men, the man Christ Jesus, **who gave himself as a ransom for all**, which is the testimony given at the proper time. For this I was appointed a preacher and an apostle (I am telling the truth, I am not lying), a teacher of the Gentiles in faith and truth. (1 Tim. 2:3–7)

I want to make sure I also compare 1 Timothy 2:6,

> Who gave himself as a ransom for all, which is
> the testimony given at the proper time.

With Mark 14:24,

> And he said to them, "This is my blood of the
> covenant, which is poured out **for many**."

The question arises: did Jesus die for all people—as 1 Timothy 2:6 offers—or for a subset of all—"for many" as Jesus says within Mark 14:24?

I see scripture saying both, but not in application of both. As we just saw in Timothy as with, and in part, the "Building Is on Fire" analogy, salvation is an open call to all peoples everywhere, and, unto our own heart, we reject the call. Thus, the open call explained to Timothy is to preach the Gospel to all, which is not limited just to Jews but to all peoples.

And in effectiveness of the new covenant, Jesus saves all peoples that the Father has prepared for Him to save, both from within the Jews and the Gentiles—the other sheep of His flock.

> And I have other sheep that are not of this fold. I
> must bring them also, and they will listen to my
> voice. So there will be one flock, one shepherd.
> (John 10:16)

Or some may still ask how "fair" would that be if not all men have an equal chance to be saved?

God states He will NEVER turn away anyone who seeks after Him. NEVER.

But as we have discussed, natural man cannot seek after God without the aid of the Holy Spirit within them, so the condition of God's desires of man's actions toward repentance is His desire and not His will.

> O Jerusalem, Jerusalem, the city that kills the prophets and stones those who are sent to it! How often would I have gathered your children together as a hen gathers her brood under her wings, and you were not willing! Behold, your house is forsaken. And I tell you, you will not see me until you say, "Blessed is he who comes in the name of the Lord!" (Luke 13:34–35)

Wow, prophecy—Jesus is revealing to us a time in the future that all Israel will come to faith in Christ! Jesus laments over Israel about their ignorance of God and the sin they do, and that they will not see Jesus for who He is until they acknowledge Him and bless Him.

God's will is perfect; God desires every man to respond to Him in repentance and faith. God sends Jesus to save the world. No man comes to Jesus, because all men are blinded by sin, until God's Spirit opens the heart to the wisdom of the Gospel. God saves those He wills. God is fair to God.

A closing analogy...

My Will and My Desire for My Children Compared

Another weak analogy. This time my hope is to show the difference between my will for my kids and my desires. Sometimes, to see God's perspective, it may help to find a word picture that we can relate to. Again, God is big, real big, and His ways are not our ways, but I believe it is especially important to pursue after God to know Him as He reveals and enables us to find Him.

As a parent, my <u>desire</u> is that my kids make good choices in life, that they seek to do good, and that they be at the best in all things unto the Lord.

My <u>will</u> for them, which I try to accomplish through my effort, is to train them up in the ways of the Lord, to supply the background of education, of provision while at home to care for them, and of the like.

Now this also has points of analogy failure, for if I teach them the ways of the Lord, they may not want to learn, while God gives us a new heart that we want to learn His ways.

But in loose comparison, the focus is on me with a parent's point of view. I will and act to pay for their college education; my desire is that they do well. I will and act to teach them about Jesus and life; my desire is that they take it to heart. Now back to God. God's will, will be done, for there is no plan B. God's desire is for every man to repent. Only those that He grants (wills) repentance to will repent, all others will not. See the difference between God's will and desire.

Again, God's will is His actions. God's desires are placed upon others in response to Him, so to speak. His will is never thwarted. His desires, given the fallen nature of man, are rarely, if at all, fulfilled.

Now to understand "man's will" a bit better…

4

Free Will = Willing Choices?

The heart of man plans his way, but the Lord establishes his steps. (Prov. 16:9)

A.W. Pink God's Sovereignty and the Human Will

What is the Will [of man]? We answer, the will is the faculty of choice, the immediate cause of all action. Choice necessarily implies the refusal of one thing and the acceptance of another. The positive and the negative must both be present to the mind before there can be any choice. In every act of the will there is preference, the desiring of one thing rather than another. Where there is no preference, but complete indifference, there is no volition. To will is to choose, and to choose is to decide between alternatives. But there is something which influences the choice; something which determines the decision. Hence the will cannot be sovereign because it is the servant of that something. The will cannot be both sovereign and servant. It cannot be both cause and effect. The will is not causative, because, as we have said, something causes it to choose; therefore that something must be the causative agent. Choice itself is affected by certain considerations, is determined by various influences brought to bear upon the individual himself; hence, volition is the effect of these considerations and influences, and if the effect, it must be their servant; and if the will is their servant then it is not sovereign, and if the will is not sovereign, we certainly cannot predicate absolute "freedom" of it. Acts of the will cannot come to pass of themselves—to say they can, is to postulate an uncaused effect. "Ex nihilo nihil fit"—out of nothing, nothing comes.[2]

God has gifted man with the abilities of thought, and in thought, we think all sorts of things, do we not? I open this chapter quoting A.W. Pink with his thoughts regarding man's will and, in part, man's ability to think. But I reordered the full quote from Pink to begin with his definition first and his logic second. Here is Pink's logic of the first part of his comments to the object of the second part now being second within his writings, as you scratch your head in wonder what is my point:

> Let us appeal to the actual experience of the Christian reader. Was there not a time (may the remembrance of it bow each of us into the dust!) when you were unwilling to come to Christ? There was. Since then you have come to Him. Are you now prepared to give Him all the glory for that (Psalms 115:1)? Do You acknowledge you came to Christ because the Holy Spirit brought you from unwillingness to willingness? You do. Then is it not also a patent fact that the

2   A. W. Pink, "The Nature of the Human Will," *God's Sovereignty and the Human Will*.

Holy Spirit has not done in many others what He has in you? Granted that many others have heard the Gospel, been shown their need of Christ; yet they are still unwilling to come to Him. Thus He has wrought more in you than in them. Do you answer, Yet I remember well the time when the Great Issue was presented to me, and my consciousness testifies that my will acted and that I yielded to the claims of Christ upon me. Quite true! But before you "yielded," the Holy Spirit overcame the native enmity of your mind against God, and this "enmity" He does not overcome in all. Should it be said, That is because they are unwilling for their enmity to be overcome—ah, none are thus "willing" till He has put forth His almighty power and wrought a miracle of grace in the heart.[3]

It was my goal and purpose to show that free will, as many would define, leaves the determination to man as a product of his thinking—logic. But as Pink writes, man's logic is flawed, primarily based on sin and on being finite created man.

Thus, God must step in; He must write upon the heart. He must open the heart and shine the glory of the Gospel within us, and He must instruct the heart to understand and respond, now adding—willingly responding on our part.

Either Slave to Sin or Slave to Righteousness—John 8:34 | Romans 6:17

Jesus answered them, "Truly, truly, I say to you, everyone who practices sin is a slave to sin." (John 8:34)

---

[3] A. W. Pink, "The Nature of the Human Will," *God's Sovereignty and the Human Will*.

> But thanks be to God, that you who were once slaves of sin have become obedient from the heart to the standard of teaching to which you were committed, and, having been set free from sin, have become slaves of righteousness. I am speaking in human terms, because of your natural limitations. For just as you once presented your members as slaves to impurity and to lawlessness leading to more lawlessness, so now present your members as slaves to righteousness leading to sanctification. (Rom. 6:17–19)

Jesus bluntly states that if you practice sin—meaning if you willfully think, then pursue, and then commit sin, you find little if any fault within sinning—then you are a slave to it. But God, through Jesus, sets us free from sin! If indeed Jesus now lives within you, see Romans 8:1–11.

Rabbit trail #1

I hope you can now see that God changes our hearts of stone to hearts of flesh, and He writes His precepts upon our hearts to know Him, to love Him, and to be obedient to him. And He awakens us prior to our coming to Him in faith, whether a microsecond or minutes before our understanding the Gospel.

For your consideration, I now submit that in being saved, God also changes our hearts and our requests through prayers. For example, when David sees his sin against God from God's perspective, knowing the sin of his heart, he then asks God to forgive him and to change him:

> Have mercy on me, O God, according to your steadfast love; according to your abundant mercy blot out my transgressions. **Wash me thoroughly from my iniquity, and cleanse me from my sin! For I know my transgressions, and my sin is ever**

**before me. Against you, you only, have I sinned
and done what is evil in your sight, so that you
may be justified in your words and blameless
in your judgment.** Behold, I was brought forth
in iniquity, and in sin did my mother conceive
me. Behold, you delight in truth in the inward
being, and you teach me wisdom in the secret
heart. Purge me with hyssop, and I shall be clean;
wash me, and I shall be whiter than snow. Let me
hear joy and gladness; let the bones that you have
broken rejoice. Hide your face from my sins, and
blot out all my iniquities. <u>Create in me a clean
heart, O God, and renew a right spirit within
me</u>. Cast me not away from your presence, and
take not your Holy Spirit from me. Restore to me
the joy of **your salvation**, and uphold me with a
willing spirit. (Ps. 51:1–12)

For now that God has saved us, we through Christ are in relationship with Him, and we should be walking and talking with Him,
like breathing—inhaling the word of God and exhaling in prayer and
supplication to Him—whereas the Holy Spirit convicts us of our
sins, for us to see and to respond to Him, He guides us to repentance.
AND God also is able to keep us from sinning, in accordance with
His will!

Jesus even teaches us to ask God for forgiveness AND to also ask
that God would keep us from sinning.

And forgive us our debts, as we also have forgiven
our debtors. And lead us not into temptation,
but deliver us from evil. (Matt. 6:12–13)

And again, God does this for HIS glory, HIS name's sake, and as
a result, for our benefit.
PRAISE GOD!

> Now to him who is able to keep you from stumbling and to present you blameless before the presence of his glory with great joy, to the only God, our Savior, through Jesus Christ our Lord, be glory, majesty, dominion, and authority, before all time and now and forever. Amen. (Jude 1:24–25)

How many times have you had thoughts of sinning and, in weakness, you followed through? And, oh, how many times have you had thoughts about sinning, and for some reason, it was thwarted? To God be the glory, He saved you from that moment of sinning! He can and does hold us from sinning by the counsel of His will! Now knowing that God can keep you from sinning, will your prayer life be different going forward? "O Father, keep me from the temptations that are weak within me, for Your glory and name's sake I ask, so that my joy is in you and not within the sin I considered."

Choice Making

In Psalm 139, David seeks to understand who God is in relation to himself. This one psalm reveals so much wisdom as to God's revealed character, and man's frailty considering his Creator, and to the nature of salvation in the light of God as experienced by David.

So as I look throughout the Bible, God, writing through the hands of the prophets and disciples, calls for making choices of actively following. One of the most recognizable verses with this action call is found in Joshua 24:15:

> And if it is evil in your eyes to serve the Lord, choose this day whom you will serve, whether the gods your fathers served in the region beyond the River, or the gods of the Amorites in whose land you dwell. **But as for me and my house, we will serve the Lord.**

This verse is engraved on a wooden plaque that I have placed high upon the threshold of our first front arch from the front door. I see this as a reminder—to me, my family, and to anyone who enters—that our house is a house of the Lord. Did I choose to place that plaque there? Yes. Did I choose to serve the Lord? Yes. But does my choice both in believing scripture or hanging it above the threshold drive God to respond to me? No. it is just the opposite. I am responding to God.

Order of Salvation: Does Believing First Make You "Born Again" or Does Being Born Again Precede Believing?

First an illustration: Two men, Bill and John, attend church with their wives every Sunday. And each Sunday, the Gospel of Jesus Christ is faithfully preached. Now both men attend because it pleases their wives, and by self-profession (choice), they are not "saved." Every Sunday they hear the Gospel of Christ, and both men leave church at the end of the service, shaking the pastor's hand, and then go to lunch with their wives.

This continues for ten years, and nothing changes each Sunday. They get up, get dressed, go to church, hear the gospel, shake the pastor's hand, and go to lunch.

But one Sunday, something different happens. Bill hears the pastor preach the Gospel again, but this time, something happens. He hears the Gospel again, the same Gospel he has heard preached over 520 times before, but it is different this time. Tears begin welling up in his eyes as the pastor is preaching the Word of God, and Bill, hearing the Gospel one more time, now says, "I believe"—or maybe I should use "I accept Jesus into my heart," as many folks profess. It does not matter. Bill just responds to the Gospel this day.

John, on the other hand, shook the pastor's hand and went to lunch with his wife. Two men, hearing the same Gospel for 521 times, Bill hears and believes on this day, and John hears and, for the lack of a better word, nothing. How can this be? Both having "free wills," both hearing the Gospel, one chooses to "accept" and believe, and the other does not choose anything this day. Why?

What changed in Bill? Why did he now accept the Gospel this day? And why didn't John respond as Bill did? Something changed. But what?

So salvation is of the Lord, and it is a gift of His grace and His faith given to those who believe: the opening of the eyes of the heart in His wisdom and the testifying through His spirit to our spirit that we are His. For previously the god of this world had blinded our hearts to the light of the Gospel of the grace of God in the works of Jesus Christ. The order of being saved is to be born again first by GOD's Spirit, who first removes the blinders of understanding to the truth of the Gospel. The Spirit works within the heart of the believer, and the same Holy Spirit works within the heart and mouth of the one preaching the Gospel: God miraculously spiritually births a believer to the wisdom of God in salvation.

Understanding you are a sinner, a sinner that can't earn salvation; that you see God as holy, pure, and sinless; and His Son as the propitiation (atonement or full payment) for your sins, past, present, and future, to lead us to say that in faith—given of God through Jesus as testified by the Holy Spirit, with repentance (agreeing with God and turning away from sin and toward God)—granted and taught by God, to understand/acknowledge/act, we see, we repent, we believe (or as some say, accept), and we glorify Christ in the gift of God's salvation applied to us.

> God's "sealing" (Ephesians 1:13)—his decisive, keeping influence—does not turn us into machines. It keeps us safe in the worship of God forever. No one who is justified will fail to be glorified (Romans 8:30). Heaven will never see an insurrection among the saints. Not because we are better than the angels, but because the blood of Jesus secured the new covenant for God's elect, where God says, "I will put the fear of me in their hearts, that they may not turn from me"

(Jeremiah 32:40). He bought this pledge for his
children by his blood. They will not commit
treason. Let us praise such sovereign, merciful,
keeping influence. God save us from slandering
his saving power. (John Piper[4])

Bill and John were real acquaintances, and I saw God work in
the hearts of both men, but at different times. I share their story,
not as a pattern but to show the sovereignty of God in His calling.
Remember that man's salvation is for God, of God, by God, in God,
through God, because of God, and for the Glory of God, lest any
man would boast.

Does God Limit Himself to Man Choosing Him First?

In a word, no. Going back to the reorder of scripture section, it
is my hope and desire to reinforce that God instills the new covenant
that He makes with Himself and with those He has called to faith. I
realize that I am being a bit repetitive, but it is so important to grasp
that God changes hearts for us. What wonderful news!

So what follows is a grouping of scripture as written within the
Bible that points to God's working with us whom He called to faith
in Jesus. At the end, I will take key points from each reference and
build the same position with very few words on my part, as my effort
to connect the dots, but again I pray that the Holy Spirit will grant
you the wisdom to see.

Behold, the days are coming, declares the Lord,
when I will make a new covenant with the house
of Israel and the house of Judah, not like the covenant that I made with their fathers on the day
when I took them by the hand to bring them
out of the land of Egypt, my covenant that they

---

[4] Ibid.

broke, though I was their husband, declares the Lord. For this is the covenant that I will make with the house of Israel after those days, declares the Lord: I will put my law within them, and I will write it on their hearts. And I will be their God, and they shall be my people. (Jer. 31:31–33)

And he took bread, and when he had given thanks, he broke it and gave it to them, saying, "This is my body, which is given for you. Do this in remembrance of me." And likewise the cup after they had eaten, saying, "This cup that is poured out for you is the new covenant in my blood." (Luke 22:19–20)

In the same way also he took the cup, after supper, saying, "This cup is the new covenant in my blood. Do this, as often as you drink it, in remembrance of me." (1 Cor. 11:25)

Are we beginning to commend ourselves again? Or do we need, as some do, letters of recommendation to you, or from you? You yourselves are our letter of recommendation, written on our hearts, to be known and read by all. And you show that you are a letter from Christ delivered by us, written not with ink but with the Spirit of the living God, not on tablets of stone but on tablets of human hearts. Such is the confidence that we have through Christ toward God. Not that we are sufficient in ourselves to claim anything as coming from us, but our sufficiency is from God, who has made us sufficient to be ministers of a new covenant, not of the letter but of the Spirit. For the letter kills, but the Spirit gives life. (2 Cor. 3:1–6)

But as it is, Christ has obtained a ministry that is as much more excellent than the old as the covenant he mediates is better, since it is enacted on better promises. For if that first covenant had been faultless, there would have been no occasion to look for a second. For he finds fault with them when he says: "Behold, the days are coming, declares the Lord, when I will establish a new covenant with the house of Israel and with the house of Judah, not like the covenant that I made with their fathers on the day when I took them by the hand to bring them out of the land of Egypt. For they did not continue in my covenant, and so I showed no concern for them, declares the Lord. For this is the covenant that I will make with the house of Israel after those days, declares the Lord: I will put my laws into their minds, and write them on their hearts, and I will be their God, and they shall be my people." (Heb. 8:6–10)

But it is not as though the word of God has failed. For not all who are descended from Israel belong to Israel, and not all are children of Abraham because they are his offspring, but "Through Isaac shall your offspring be named." This means that it is not the children of the flesh who are the children of God, but the children of the promise are counted as offspring. (Rom. 9:6–8)

Therefore he is the mediator of a new covenant, so that those who are called may receive the promised eternal inheritance, since a death has occurred that redeems them from the transgressions committed under the first covenant. (Heb. 9:15)

And the Lord said to Paul one night in a vision, "Do not be afraid, but go on speaking and do not be silent, for I am with you, and no one will attack you to harm you, for I have many in this city who are my people." (Acts 18:9–10)

And I will give you a new heart, and a new spirit I will put within you. And I will remove the heart of stone from your flesh and give you a heart of flesh. And I will put my Spirit within you, and cause you to walk in my statutes and be careful to obey my rules. (Ezek. 36:26–27)

But this is what was uttered through the prophet Joel: "And in the last days it shall be, God declares, that I will pour out my Spirit on all flesh, and your sons and your daughters shall prophesy, and your young men shall see visions, and your old men shall dream dreams; even on my male servants and female servants in those days I will pour out my Spirit, and they shall prophesy." (Acts 2:16–18)

The Lord Will Pour Out His Spirit

And it shall come to pass afterward, that I will pour out my Spirit on all flesh; your sons and your daughters shall prophesy, your old men shall dream dreams, and your young men shall see visions. Even on the male and female servants in those days I will pour out my Spirit. (Joel 2:28–29)

Now taking the scriptures from above and cutting, copying, and pasting them together as to be written as one thought—one big quote, so to speak—here is a glimpse into how my hermeneutics works within my heart and mind:

The LORD your God will circumcise your heart and the heart of your offspring, so that you will love the LORD your God with all your heart and with all your soul, that you may live. [For] "Behold, the days are coming, declares the Lord, when I will make a new covenant with the house of Israel and the house of Judah, not like the covenant that I made with their fathers on the day when I took them by the hand to bring them out of the land of Egypt, my covenant that they broke, though I was their husband, declares the Lord. For this is the covenant that I will make with the house of Israel after those days, declares the Lord: I will put my law within them, and I will write it on their hearts. And I will be their God, and they shall be my people." For not all who are descended from Israel belong to Israel, and not all are children of Abraham because they are his offspring, but "Through Isaac shall your offspring be named." This means that it is not the children of the flesh who are the children of God, but the children of the promise are counted as offspring.

And I will give you a new heart, and a new spirit I will put within you. And I will remove the heart of stone from your flesh and give you a heart of flesh. And I will put my Spirit within you, and cause you to walk in my statutes and be careful to obey my rules. And you show that you are a letter from Christ delivered by us [Paul], written not with ink but with the Spirit of the living God, not on tablets of stone but on tablets of human hearts.

Therefore he [Jesus] is the mediator of a new covenant, so that those who are called may receive the promised eternal inheritance, since a death has occurred that redeems them from the transgressions committed under the first covenant. To all who did receive him, who believed in his name, he gave the right to become children of God, who were born, not of blood nor of the will of the flesh nor of the will of man, but of God.

Everyone who believes that Jesus is the Christ has been born of God, and everyone who loves the Father loves whoever has been born of him.

And he [Jesus] took bread, and when he had given thanks, he broke it and gave it to them, saying, "This is my body, which is given for you. Do this in remembrance of me." And likewise the cup after they had eaten, saying, "This cup that is poured out for you is the new covenant in my blood."

[Repeating for emphasis]

And I will give you a new heart, and a new spirit I will put within you. And I will remove the heart of stone from your flesh and give you a heart of flesh. And I will put my Spirit within you, and cause you to walk in my statutes and be careful to obey my rules.

I trust that for some, this helps see that the sum of the word is truth and that removing the verse reference and rearranging the order is like a jigsaw puzzle—every piece having a precise part, and each part has a precise location, and all parts together give the picture. Again my goal is not to take anything out of context but to bring into focus the precept upon precept of the Word of God.

For it is precept upon precept, precept upon precept, line upon line, line upon line, here a little, there a little. (Isa. 28:10)

But Some May Ask, "What about Resisting the Holy Spirit?"

Or grieving the Holy Spirit? Yes, this does happen. But God, when according to His will, by His Spirit, He "messes" with our heart by revealing and then enabling the light of the gospel to penetrate our heart, all the while the Gospel now becomes our possession, our action—to agree with God and believe God. Going back to "'The House Is on Fire' Analogy" of Chapter 1, with the blinders now removed and the truth now making sense, who would not believe? Not talking coercion, not talking against one's "will" going kicking and screaming into salvation, but a humble realization that God loves you and that He purposed to go after you and save you. He comes to you and loves you, and you see that God is the only one who can save you. Now that the fireman has awakened you from a sound sleep, who would then tell the fireman upon awakening, "No, thank you"?

Man can resist the Holy Spirit, but God overcomes the resistance anytime He so wills. So from the day of one's birth to the day of being born again, and even to the day of one's death, all three events are now known, as with each day in life, that they are ordained by God. God gives life, and He also takes life. And in salvation when He gives eternal life, it is for keeps. For salvation of any man is…for God, of God, by God, in God, through God, because of God, and for the Glory of God, lest any man would boast.

A journey back into Romans 9

> For the Lord will not cast off forever, but, though he cause grief, **he will have compassion according to the abundance of his steadfast love**; for he does not afflict from his heart or grieve the children of men. (Lam. 3:31–33)

> What shall we say then? Is there injustice on God's part? By no means! For he says to Moses, "I will have mercy on whom I have mercy, and I

will have compassion on whom I have compassion." So then it depends not on human will or exertion, but on God, who has mercy. For the Scripture says to Pharaoh, "For this very purpose I have raised you up, that I might show my power in you, and that my name might be proclaimed in all the earth." So then he has mercy on whomever he wills, and he hardens whomever he wills. You will say to me then, "Why does he still find fault? For who can resist his will?" But who are you, O man, to answer back to God? Will what is molded say to its molder, "Why have you made me like this?" Has the potter no right over the clay, to make out of the same lump one vessel for honorable use and another for dishonorable use? What if God, desiring to show his wrath and to make known his power, has endured with much patience vessels of wrath prepared for destruction, in order to make known the riches of his glory for vessels of mercy, which he has prepared beforehand for glory—even us whom he has called, not from the Jews only but also from the Gentiles? (Rom. 9:14–24)

Let us reflect upon God's glory for a minute. Look at Genesis 1, Ezekiel 1, Isaiah 6, Acts 1, and Revelation 1 and 4. Imagine you are there! Would not just being in the back of the room in the presence of God be such a thrilling experience (Ps. 27:4; Ps. 23:6)? And all the while in what you would see, you would also hear the angels crying out,

Holy, holy, holy is the LORD of hosts; the whole earth is full of his glory! (Isa. 6:3)

And,

At once I was in the Spirit, and behold, a throne
stood in heaven, with one seated on the throne.
And he who sat there had the appearance of jas-
per and carnelian, and around the throne was a
rainbow that had the appearance of an emerald.
Around the throne were twenty-four thrones, and
seated on the thrones were twenty-four elders,
clothed in white garments, with golden crowns
on their heads. From the throne came flashes of
lightning, and rumblings and peals of thunder,
and before the throne were burning seven torches
of fire, which are the seven spirits of God, and
before the throne there was as it were a sea of
glass, like crystal. And around the throne, on
each side of the throne, are four living creatures,
full of eyes in front and behind: the first living
creature like a lion, the second living creature like
an ox, the third living creature with the face of a
man, and the fourth living creature like an eagle
in flight. And the four living creatures, each of
them with six wings, are full of eyes all around
and within, and day and night they never cease to
say, "Holy, holy, holy, is the Lord God Almighty,
who was and is and is to come!" And whenever
the living creatures give glory and honor and
thanks to him who is seated on the throne, who
lives forever and ever, the twenty-four elders fall
down before him who is seated on the throne and
worship him who lives forever and ever. They cast
their crowns before the throne, saying, "Worthy
are you, our Lord and God, to receive glory and
honor and power, for you created all things, and
by your will they existed and were created." (Rev.
4:2–11)

So with that as backdrop, let us investigate Romans 9.

First to note that God finds no pleasure in His punishment for sin. His standards are His standards, and they are right, pure, and holy. As I have repeated many times before, all men are sinners, and all deserve God's justice for the wages of sin.

And worthy of repeating: "For God so loved the world, that he gave his only Son, that whoever believes in him should not perish but have eternal life" (John 3:16).

But who would believe?

> And you were dead in the trespasses and sins in which you once walked, following the course of this world, following the prince of the power of the air, the spirit that is now at work in the sons of disobedience—among whom we all once lived in the passions of our flesh, carrying out the desires of the body and the mind, and were by nature children of wrath, like the rest of mankind. (Eph. 2:1–3)

But God steps in via the new covenant! As was His plan and will from before the foundation of the world. He saves those He has called as a people unto Himself, which leads to the question regarding Romans 9:14–24, as some may ask, "Is God fair?"

For which Paul responds:

> What shall we say then? Is there injustice on God's part? By no means! For he says to Moses, "I will have mercy on whom I have mercy, and I will have compassion on whom I have compassion." So then it depends not on human will or exertion, but on God, who has mercy. (Romans 9:14–16)

To the world, fairness of God can be a tough concept to grasp, for the world believes in comparison, it believes in a different value set as to right and wrong and adapts changing attitudes and values as it makes these values "relative" to culture, and many times with pragmatism, as Pink describes.

Being fair to man says to treat everyone the same. Oh, how many times can we count within the home, the workplace, and the neighborhoods and hear "That's not fair!" That the world says that treating all people the same as equal is to being fair.

For if God treated everyone the same, then all people are judged as sinners, and all people pay with their lives for the wages of their sins. Or could God simply forgive everyone their sins?

For God, being holy and having and setting the standards of holiness, righteousness, and justice and as such, He cannot even look upon sin. Sin must be paid for. For if God were fair as the world defines fair, then every man would have to pay the price for their own sins, which is death. BUT God is rich in mercy and grace and has sent His Son to pay the price for our sins once and for all, thus He is our Savior from sin, as well as our Lord and King!

So What Is Fair to Your Standards?—A Parenting Analogy

Let say I have two children: Tommy, age sixteen, and Sally, age fifteen. Both want to play outside with their friends after dinner. And both have a time they need to be back home through a curfew I have set for both. Tommy needs to be home by 10:00 p.m. and Sally needs to be in by 8:00 p.m. Is this fair?

Some of you will say yes, and some will say no. For those who say I am unfair, you may point out the age variance as being unfair on my part, and some of you may point out that I give my son a later curfew than my daughter and that would be unfair because one is a boy and the other is a girl.

We judge others and their ways all the time, for we compare others to the values, experience, and knowledge of our own minds, and not all come to the same conclusions. This also applies to "relative truth," but for now let me stay focused on perspective. The focal point of the values then of those who disagree with me is not from my perspective, their father, but of Tommy and Sally, the ones who have been given the rules by me to follow.

Let me talk a little tough here to make a point. "Hey, they are my kids, my house, my street, and my rules."

The point to note is that fairness is relatively judged within this example. You may agree with me, or you may disagree with me. For you would be applying your set of values and potentially bringing your experiences and circumstances to this story. Your point is not seeing it from my perspective but perhaps from my children's and/or your "relative" values and experiences and are either judging by age or by gender, or both, as to what is right of me in the curfew I set. (And the curfew is my love and my guidance to the individual needs of each child.)

So let me bring this back to God and His fairness to man.

God has created all things for His glory and good pleasure.

> Worthy are you, our Lord and God, to receive glory and honor and power, for you created all things, and by your will they existed and were created. (Rev. 4:11)

The Gospel is open to all who hear, but as we are learning, our minds have been blinded to sin, and the lust of an unregenerate heart does not seek after God but does what the flesh wants to do—sin.

God, being holy and righteous, has set the standards and boundaries for man and for life, and His rules of physics, rules of life, and rules of law are the standard for all men to live by. And all men fail. Yet God does not enjoy punishing man for man's unrighteousness, but He must have sin accounted for, for the wages of sin is death. All men are condemned because of sin.

So God is to man in this story as I am to my children. My rules for Tommy and Sally are to God's rules to you and me. (I have left out if Tommy and Sally were obedient to the rules I set for them on purpose—for the point I wanted to make was about God's standards and His will and not about obedience, which I acknowledge is also important to God.)

God is fair to God. God is MORE than fair to man. For God gives grace. The world did not care or even listen. He gave the world His Son, and each man has no excuse but to repent and believe,

> [For] if you confess with your mouth that Jesus is Lord and believe in your heart that God raised him from the dead, you will be saved. For with the heart one believes and is justified, and with the mouth one confesses and is saved. For the Scripture says, "Everyone who believes in him will not be put to shame." For there is no distinction between Jew and Greek; for the same Lord is Lord of all, bestowing his riches on all who call on him. For "everyone who calls on the name of the Lord will be saved." (Rom. 10:9–13)

And when you believe, know that it was God's working with your heart to believe, and now you should be able to start to focus in on humbly seeing His purpose for you, and His plan of salvation birthed within you, in plan and in view from before the time of creation to the date your eyes saw His glory and your sin, and then to realize that Jesus is yours. The chains of sin have been broken in your life, the glory of the Lord now shining so brightly within your heart and mind.

Because your salvation is…

5

For God, of God, by God, in God, through God, because of God, and for the Glory of God, Lest Any Man Would Boast

But you are a chosen race, a royal priesthood, a holy nation, a people for his own possession, that you may proclaim the excellencies of him who called you out of darkness into his marvelous light. Once you were not a people, but now you are God's people; once you had not received mercy, but now you have received mercy. (1 Pet. 2:9–10)

For consider your calling, brothers: not many of you were wise according to worldly standards, not many were powerful, not many were of noble birth. **But God chose** what is foolish in the world to shame the wise; **God chose** what is weak in the world to shame the strong; **God chose** what is low and despised in the world, even things that are not, to bring to nothing things that are, <u>so that no human being might boast in the presence of God</u>. And <u>because of him you are in Christ Jesus, who became to us wisdom from God, righteousness, sanctification, and redemption</u>, so that, as it is written, "Let the one who boasts, boast in the Lord." (1 Cor. 1:26–31)

He is the image of the invisible God, the first-born of all creation. For by him all things were created, in heaven and on earth, visible and invisible, whether thrones or dominions or rulers or authorities—all things were created through him and for him. And he is before all things, and in him all things hold together. And he is the head of the body, the church. He is the beginning, the firstborn from the dead, that in everything he might be preeminent. For in him all the fullness of God was pleased to dwell, and through him to reconcile to himself all things, whether on earth or in heaven, making peace by the blood of his cross. (Col. 1:15–20)

All things were made through him, and without him was not any thing made that was made. (John 1:3)

God Works within Us for His Glory—God's Sanctification in Us

Blessed be the God and Father of our Lord Jesus Christ! According to his great mercy, he has caused us to be born again to a living hope through the resurrection of Jesus Christ from the dead, to an inheritance that is imperishable, undefiled, and unfading, kept in heaven for you, who by God's power are being guarded through faith for a salvation ready to be revealed in the last time. (1 Pet. 1:3–5)

Now to him who is able to keep you from stumbling and to present you blameless before the presence of his glory with great joy, to the only God, our Savior, through Jesus Christ our Lord, be glory, majesty, dominion, and authority, before all time and now and forever. Amen. (Jude 1:24–25)

Now may the God of peace himself sanctify you completely, and may your whole spirit and soul and body be kept blameless at the coming of our Lord Jesus Christ. He who calls you is faithful; he will surely do it. (1 Thess. 5:23–24)

And I am sure of this, that he who began a good work in you will bring it to completion at the day of Jesus Christ. (Phil. 1:6)

So that you are not lacking in any gift, as you wait for the revealing of our Lord Jesus Christ, who will sustain you to the end, guiltless in the day of our Lord Jesus Christ. God is faithful, by whom you were called into the fellowship of his Son, Jesus Christ our Lord. (1 Cor. 1:7–9)

Now may the God of peace who brought again from the dead our Lord Jesus, the great shepherd of the sheep, by the blood of the eternal covenant, equip you with everything good that you may do his will, working in us that which is pleasing in his sight, through Jesus Christ, to whom be glory forever and ever. Amen. (Heb. 13:20–21)

Our salvation is all God's work, and working through the new covenant toward us, we see examples through scripture of His working within us, to the glory of His grace.

For "He has caused us to be born again," "to a living hope through the resurrection of Jesus Christ from the dead, to an inheritance that is imperishable, undefiled, and unfading, kept in heaven for you," "who by God's power are being guarded through faith," "who is able to keep you from stumbling," "to present you blameless before the presence of His glory," for which "He who began a good work in you will bring it to completion at the day of Jesus Christ, who will sustain you to the end, guiltless in the day of our Lord Jesus Christ," and again "God is faithful, by who you were called into fellowship of His Son, Jesus Christ, our Lord," so that "the God of Peace… Equip you with everything good that you may do His will, working in us that which is pleasing in His sight, through Jesus Christ, to who be glory forever and ever. Amen."

And certainly not last to quote, but to this chapter's focus, that Jesus, before He was to go to the cross, offers prayers to God the Father. I would love to quote chapter 17 in its entirety, for it is so rich into insight to relationships from Jesus's perspective of Jesus to God, God to Jesus; Jesus to His disciples, His disciples to Jesus; Jesus to us, us to Jesus; disciples to us, us to the disciples; and even Jesus to the world, the world to Jesus.

And a big view into the heart of Jesus toward the Father, to Himself, to the disciples, and then to us!

Jesus prays for His disciples

> **For I have given them the words that you gave me**, and **they have received them and have come to know in truth that I came from you; and they have believed that you sent me. I am praying for them**. I am not praying for the world but **for those whom you have given me, for they are yours**. All mine are yours, and yours are mine, **and I am glorified in them**. And I am no longer in the world, but they are in the world, and I am coming to you. Holy Father, **keep them in your name, which you have given me, that**

> **they may be one, even as we are one.** While
> I was with them, **I kept them in your name,**
> which you have given me. **I have guarded them,**
> and **not one of them has been lost except the
> son of destruction, that the Scripture might
> be fulfilled.** But **now I am coming to you,** and
> these things I speak in the world, **that they may
> have my joy fulfilled in themselves. I have
> given them your word,** and the world has hated
> them because they are not of the world, just as I
> am not of the world. **I do not ask that you take
> them out of the world, but that you keep them
> from the evil one.** They are not of the world,
> just as I am not of the world. **Sanctify them in
> the truth; your word is truth.** As you sent me
> into the world, so **I have sent them into the
> world.** And **for their sake I consecrate myself,
> that they also may be sanctified in truth.** (John
> 17:8–19)

Jesus asks the Father that He would "sanctify the disciples in truth." That God would work His work within them and set them apart through the truth, which is in Christ Jesus. Likewise...

Jesus then prays for us

> **I do not ask for these only, but also** for those
> who will believe in me through their word,
> [The disciples' testimony, both spoken and writ-
> ten] that **they** [those of us who believe] may all be
> one, just as you, Father, are in me, and I in you,
> that **they also may be in us, so that the world
> may believe that you have sent me.** The glory
> that you have given me I have given to them, that
> they may be one even as we are one, **I in them
> and you in me, that they may become per-**

143

fectly one, so that the world may know that you sent me and loved them even as you loved me. Father, **I desire that they also, whom you have given me, may be with me where I am, to see my glory that you have given me because you loved me before the foundation of the world.** O righteous Father, even though the world does not know you, I know you, and these know that you have sent me. I made known to them your name, and I will continue to make it known, that the love with which you have loved me may be in them, and I in them. (John 17:20–26)

Continued to…

6

God Reveals | God Enables

Open Call—Reveals to Everyone Everywhere

When God reveals, I see both an open revelation (a global call) as in Matthew 28:19–20:

> **Go therefore and make disciples of all nations, baptizing them in the name of the Father and of the Son and of the Holy Spirit, teaching them to observe all that I have commanded you. And behold, I am with you always, to the end of the age.**

Private Call—Reveals with Enablement

And a private call, one wherein God "awakens" the heart of a chosen (elect) individual to hear with understanding the Gospel.

> And even if our gospel is veiled, it is veiled to those who are perishing. In their case the god of this world has blinded the minds of the unbelievers, to keep them from seeing the light of the gospel of the glory of Christ, who is the image of God. For what we proclaim is not ourselves, but Jesus Christ as Lord, with ourselves as your

servants for Jesus' sake. For God, who said, "Let light shine out of darkness," has shone in our hearts to give the light of the knowledge of the glory of God in the face of Jesus Christ. (2 Cor. 4:3–6)

The first open call deals with God revealing Himself to all peoples through the sending of missionaries, preachers, and other disciples; printing and distributing Bibles; etc. everywhere. And within the open call, there are those for whom the Spirit times our spiritual birthday—as predetermined by God before He created all things—with our heart now cultivated by the Holy Spirit, the preaching of the Gospel becomes effective through the Holy Spirit's testifying with our spirit that Jesus is Lord.

The Spirit himself bears witness with our spirit that we are children of God, and if children, then heirs—heirs of God and fellow heirs with Christ, provided we suffer with him in order that we may also be glorified with him. (Rom. 8:16–17)

This is he who came by **water and blood— Jesus Christ**; not by the water only but by **the water and the blood**. And the Spirit is the one who *testifies*, because the Spirit is the truth. For there are **three that *testify*: the Spirit and the water and the blood; and these three agree**. If we receive the *testimony* of men, the *testimony* of God is greater, for this is the *testimony* of God that he has borne **concerning his Son. Whoever believes in the Son of God has the *testimony* in himself**. Whoever does not believe God has made him a liar, because he has not believed in the *testimony* that God has borne concerning **his Son**. And this is the *testimony*, that God gave us eternal life, **and this life is in his Son. Whoever**

has the Son has life; whoever does not have the
Son of God does not have life. (1 John 5:6–12)

Taking a Closer Look to "This Is He Who Came by Water and Blood—Jesus Christ"

John starts by writing that the water and blood, Jesus Christ, is towards us. John then writes that Jesus is called the Son with respect to God (i.e., His Son, Son of God), and then John closes this instruction by bringing His Son as our possession through the testimony into our hearts. The Spirit regenerates our hearts for the Gospel of Jesus to shine brightly within us!

John uses *testify* and *testimony* eight times within these six verses—I am thinking this is very important.

This is HE—Jesus Christ—who came by (a) the water and (b) the blood.

And not just by the water but by the water and the blood.

The Spirit is the one who testifies—why? Because the Spirit is truth.

For there are three that testify. Now there are three: (1) the Spirit, (2) the water and (3) the blood—and they all agree.

But remember John opens this section stating, "THIS IS HE who came by water and blood—that is Jesus Christ." So water and blood are representative of Jesus.

Stop for a second. John starts verse 6 with THIS IS HE, which is Jesus Christ [who came by both (a) the water and (b) the blood]. So the water and the blood is a strong reference to Jesus. Maybe even a sort of title, as Jesus is also known as the vine; Jesus is the water and the blood; Jesus is the Bread of Life; Jesus is the Word; Jesus is the narrow gate; Jesus is the Christ; and Jesus is the bridegroom. So if I may, there are three that testifies: the Holy Spirit, the birth of Jesus; water and the death of Jesus; and the blood.

If we receive the testimony of men—preachers of the Gospel.

The testimony of God is greater, for it is the Holy Spirit who writes on our heart. And the Holy Spirit is also the one who *testifies*, because the Spirit is the truth.

For the testimony of God (through the Holy Spirit) has borne within us concerning His Son, Jesus Christ, the water and the blood (the life and death of Jesus).

Whoever believes in the Son has this testimony in himself (the Holy Spirit).

On the contrary, whoever does not believe God (the testimony of Jesus and the Spirit) is a liar.

Because he has not believed in the testimony. Not the testimony but in the testimony, not believing in what God has born in him concerning Jesus, His Son.

And what is this testimony? This is that God gave us eternal life, and this life is in His Son, and know that it was God who birthed this within you, by the testimony of the Spirit—to the water and the blood, which is He, Jesus Christ.

Conversely, if you do not have the testimony born by God regarding His Son within you, you do not have life.

(Jesus is referred to by John as the water and the blood...verse 6 and through John 19:33–35, "But when they came to Jesus and saw that he was already dead, they did not break his legs. But one of the soldiers pierced his side with a spear, and at once there came out blood and water. He who saw it has borne witness—his testimony is true, and he knows that he is telling the truth—that you also may believe.")

And with this for the elect, God also enables.

> And so, from the day we heard, we have not ceased to pray for you, asking that you may be filled with the knowledge of his will in all spiritual wisdom and understanding, so as to walk in a manner worthy of the Lord, fully pleasing to him: bearing fruit in every good work and increasing in the knowledge of God. (Col. 1:9–10)

Recapping.

There is a general (open) revelation to the Gospel of salvation, and then there is a personal revelation. The open call includes seeds planted on the bare ground (parable of the sower, Matthew 13:1–17, Mark 4:1–20) within the rocky or the sandy soil that is temporal, for there is nothing to hold the seed for it to take root. But the good soil that has been tilled to accept the seed, planted within the heart that has been prepared by the Holy Spirit, accepts the seed, and it takes root and grows to produce fruit. You will remember in 2 Corinthians 4 that He is giving light where there once was darkness into our hearts, to see and understand the knowledge of the glory of God in the face of Jesus Christ. And in the personal revelation, there also is enablement. Being saved has both these works of God within you.

In chapter 5, we looked at man's salvation as being the work of God. In chapter 6, it is my hope to show how God touches those He has called.

We learned that God must actively change our hearts, and that He does so by the Holy Spirit, but many Christians have wondered how this happens, and at a point in time, so did I.

So I am going to offer my testimony again to share how this happens.

If you read my testimony, you may remember that I went to church camp as a teen, twice. Once at thirteen and again when I was fourteen. The first year I heard the Gospel preached, while God, by His Spirit within the preacher, shared openly the Gospel of Jesus. I heard it. I self-judged that by my own understandings that I was saved at that time, so nothing to say more than I had a good time at camp.

However, the second year, I heard the Gospel again, and something happened. It was not a physical reaction at first but an intellectual understanding that awakened me. I heard the Gospel again, but this time something clicked. It is like the blinders or fog that was removed for me, and I saw Jesus and His love being applied to me, and that my sin, which also became real to me, was before my eyes like it has not been before. Then this understanding, the wisdom of salvation, turned into the emotion of repentance unto forgiveness and then to the physical, of the tears welling up in my eyes now seeing the glory of MY Lord and Savior! And I cried out, "Thank you, Jesus. I believe and ask you to forgive me and to 'come into

149

my heart'!" (Although I now understand that His Spirit was already working in my heart.)

So what happened? In salvation, as well as now with our walking in salvation, God does two things: He reveals and He enables. He took my heart of stone; He removed the darkness due to Satan blocking my eyes from seeing the glory of Christ until that night! Praise God! My sin was shown to me for what it was, as sin, and through the power of the Gospel with the Holy Spirit's shining within my new heart, I believed!

I was once lost but now have been found, by the Great Shepherd who pursued me, who saved me, and now I am able to see Him as He sees me, and we are in love. This may sound a bit awkward for some, but the old children's Sunday school song is rightfully true: "Jesus loves me, this I know [for His Spirit changed my heart—you know, removed my blinders and gave me eyes that I now can see and ears that can hear], for the Bible tells me [that is what happened in my new birth] so."

And because He first loved me, and He sought me, and He bought me (with His blood); and now I willingly, humbly, and graciously love Him back, my Savior, my Lord, my King!

Paul's Letters to the Churches

If you examine the apostle Paul's letters to the many churches that he started and was involved with, you can see he opens and closes those letters with prayers that asked God to grant them wisdom of the Gospel of Christ. That God would fill them with knowledge and the truth of the Gospel. For example, let us look a bit closer to Paul's prayer for the church at Ephesus. Paul begins his letter in telling them he is praying for them and asking God...

> That the God of our Lord Jesus Christ, the Father
> of glory, may give you the Spirit of wisdom and
> of revelation in the knowledge of him, having
> the eyes of your hearts enlightened, that you may
> know what is the hope to which he has called

> you, what are the riches of his glorious inheri-
> tance in the saints, and what is the immeasurable
> greatness of his power toward us who believe,
> according to the working of his great might.
> (Eph. 1:17–19)

[See a connection? "It is written in the Prophets, and they will all be taught by God." "Everyone who has heard and learned from the Father comes to me" (John 6:45). Paul is asking God to save many at Ephesus.]

There is so much to glean from this prayer. For within three verses, a partial sentence of Paul's prayer, we can see a "whole bunch" of things:

- Asking (praying) God the Father of glory and of our Lord Jesus Christ
- To give them the spirit of wisdom
- To "reveal" and enable them the knowledge of God and of Jesus (salvation)
- Given them eyes to see; changing hearts to believe
- So that they may know the hope of their calling (assurance)

Now seeing the riches of His glory applied toward them and the immeasurable greatness of His power to us who believe (seeing the glory of God), all in accordance with His will, working of His great might.

Let us look at the Church of Philippi and another prayer of Paul's

> I thank my God in all my remembrance of you,
> always in every prayer of mine for you all making
> my prayer with joy, because of your partnership
> in the gospel from the first day until now. And I
> am sure of this, that <u>he who began a good work
> in you will bring it to completion at the day of
> Jesus Christ</u>. It is right for me to feel this way
> about you all, because I hold you in my heart, for

you are all partakers with me of grace, both in my imprisonment and in the defense and confirmation of the gospel. For God is my witness, how I yearn for you all with the affection of Christ Jesus. And <u>it is my prayer that your love may abound more and more, with knowledge and all discernment</u>, so that you may approve what is excellent, and so be pure and blameless for the day of Christ, <u>filled with the fruit of righteousness that comes through Jesus Christ, to the glory and praise of God</u>. (Phil. 1:3–11)

Look at what Paul is praying for and how it touches God, asking God to give them more grace and love and knowledge and wisdom—discernment, so that their walk would be pure and blameless—all to the praise and glory of God!

And one more...

First, <u>I thank my God through Jesus Christ for all of you</u>, because your faith is proclaimed in all the world. For God is my witness, whom I serve with my spirit in the gospel of his Son, that without ceasing I mention you always in my prayers, <u>asking that somehow by God's will I may now at last succeed in coming to you</u>. For I long to see you, that I may impart to you some spiritual gift to strengthen you—that is, <u>that we may be mutually encouraged by each other's faith, both yours and mine</u>. I do not want you to be unaware, brothers, that I have often intended to come to you (but thus far have been prevented), in order that I may reap some harvest among you as well as among the rest of the Gentiles. I am under obligation both to Greeks and to barbarians, both to the wise and to the foolish. So I am

eager to preach the gospel to you also who are in
Rome. (Rom. 1:8–15)

Paul is thanking God for their faith, and that their faith is well-known around the world! He tells them that they are always in his prayers, that he is asking God if He would grant Paul the opportunity to visit them, for in the past it wasn't within God's will for him to visit Rome, that he desires to encourage each other (fellowship) by their mutual faith in Christ, and that he'd like to preach the Gospel within Rome.

For me, these three prayers, among many others that Paul and Peter offer, sparks within me to self-examine my prayer life a little closer. To ask God to change more of my heart toward His will and less from my own self-centered desires in life.

The Lives of Peter, Paul, and Mary

God's declared roles of His choice for their lives.

Have you ever thought about the body of Christ, to the point that not all people are arms or all are legs? Meaning, that God created all people special unto themselves as He has gifted some people with a great musical voice, others with the abilities of construction, and others for a unique purpose in time? In general, have you ever thought about who you are and where you are and what you do and how you do life is unique to just you? And if so, that your purpose is gifted to you, to the glory of God.

Peter—what about John?

Which brings me to the apostle Peter. Of anyone of the disciples, I can so relate to Peter. For I aspire to be like Paul in his wisdom of salvation; be in tune to the glory of Christ like John knowing Jesus as he did; and be as structured as Luke was as he wrote about Paul, Barnabas, and John Mark's missionary journeys as well as his giving of himself in testifying with Paul about Christ. But it is Peter who I seem to relate with best. For one minute He was focused on Christ, the next minute, his focus takes him back to self.

But my point is that God has a unique purpose and plan for all people and to Peter; Jesus challenges Peter for his love.

> When they had finished breakfast, Jesus said to Simon Peter, "Simon, son of John, do you love me more than these?" He said to him, "Yes, Lord; you know that I love you." He said to him, "Feed my lambs." He said to him a second time, "Simon, son of John, do you love me?" He said to him, "Yes, Lord; you know that I love you." He said to him, "Tend my sheep." He said to him the third time, "Simon, son of John, do you love me?" Peter was grieved because he said to him the third time, "Do you love me?" and he said to him, "Lord, you know everything; you know that I love you." Jesus said to him, "Feed my sheep. Truly, truly, I say to you, when you were young, you used to dress yourself and walk wherever you wanted, but when you are old, you will stretch out your hands, and another will dress you and carry you where you do not want to go." (This he said to show by what kind of death he was to glorify God.) And after saying this he said to him, "Follow me." (John 21:15–19)

Take a closer look at the above verses. Jesus, who knows Peter inside and out, asks Peter for his love, not once, not twice, but three times. And what was Peter's response? "Lord, you know everything." (Hold onto the word *know* for chapter 7 and foreknowledge.) May I suggest that Jesus loved Peter right where Peter was, for then Jesus also was preparing Peter to go where Jesus was going to take him, by dying for Him to glorify God!

And in hearing that, Peter's "focuser" went askew again and look what happens next:

> Peter turned and saw the disciple whom Jesus loved following them, the one who also had leaned back against him during the supper and had said, "Lord, who is it that is going to betray you?" When Peter saw him, he said to Jesus, "Lord, what about this man?" Jesus said to him, "If it is my will that he remain until I come, what is that to you? You follow me!" (John 21:20–22)

"If it is my will that he remains until I come, what is that to you? You follow me!" Jesus told Peter. Jesus has a role for Peter and a role for John. John has a role that is different from Peter. As love comes into focus, their choice was melting into Christ's choice for them to step into.

Jesus—Question: "Do you love me?"

Peter—Answer: "Lord, you know everything; you know that I love you."

Jesus—Task given: "Feed my sheep."

Jesus—Prophecy that Peter will die for his faith in Christ: "To glorify God."

Peter—Question: "What about John?"

Jesus—Reply: "Worry about Peter. I have other plans for John."

What about Paul?

> But the Lord said to him [Ananias], "Go, for he [Saul/Paul] is a chosen instrument of mine to carry my name before the Gentiles and kings and the children of Israel. For I will show him how much he must suffer for the sake of my name." (Acts 9:15–16)

Saul, now named Paul, was then quick to see Jesus as the Christ ("And immediately he proclaimed Jesus in the synagogues, saying, 'He is the Son of God'" [Acts 9:20]). Jesus taught Paul all about Himself and about his mission to spread the Gospel.

Jesus sought Saul, Jesus shares the Gospel with the now named Paul, and Paul believes and is changed forever!

But after that day on the road to Damascus, Saul was changed forever. However, about that day, what does Paul declare?

> But when he who had set me apart before I was born, and who called me by his grace, was pleased to reveal his Son to me, in order that I might preach him among the Gentiles, I did not immediately consult with anyone; nor did I go up to Jerusalem to those who were apostles before me, but I went away into Arabia, and returned again to Damascus. (Gal. 1:15–17)

God set him apart…before Paul was born, leading to his being called [to the glory] of God's grace, who revealed Jesus to him, so that Paul can be a preacher to the Gentiles, by the will of God!

And as Paul, his work is laid out before him to not just discover but to walk in faith that God has prepared for him to walk in. "Go, for he is a chosen instrument of mine to carry my name before the Gentiles and kings and the children of Israel" (Acts 9:15). Paul continues to declare within his letters to the churches that he is an apostle of Christ by the will of God and that he no longer stands on his credentials as a highly educated Jew, self-described:

> Though I myself have reason for confidence in the flesh also. If anyone else thinks he has reason for confidence in the flesh, I have more: circumcised on the eighth day, of the people of Israel, of the tribe of Benjamin, a Hebrew of Hebrews; as to the law, a Pharisee; as to zeal, a persecutor of the church; as to righteousness under the law,

blameless. But whatever gain I had, I counted as loss for the sake of Christ. (Phil. 3:4–8)

"Mary, did you know?"

This is a song written in part by Mark Lowery, a former Gaither's quartet member, that speaks of the birth of Jesus, not only as the Savior of the world but of Mary as being Jesus's mother too. But more importantly, Jesus is also her Savior! Many Catholics will find fault with this statement, for they believe Mary was also sinless, being Jesus's mother according to human reasoning, but scripturally this is nowhere within the Bible.

For within the song's lyrics, Mark poignantly points out that she delivers Jesus as a baby, but Jesus came to deliver her from her sins, and for all who would believe!

Rabbit Trail #2: This song is destined to be a classic and not sure if on purpose or by accident, but musically, it patterns after the Christmas song of "What Child Is This?" I have put the two together in singing it in the past, and they fit well, both musically; both are in the same minor key as well as lyrically having the same motif.

Now back to the point of Mary being the mother of Jesus. She too was chosen of God for the role she now holds for all of eternity. No resume of qualifications given, no competition to compete against for the role, just God's sovereign choice in Mary. And Mary, being born a sinner, watched Jesus grow in wisdom and stature, as He began to teach in the synagogues about God and about Himself.

> And he said to them, "Why were you looking for me? Did you not know that I must be in my Father's house?" And they did not understand the saying that he spoke to them. And he went down with them and came to Nazareth and was submissive to them. And his mother treasured up all these things in her heart. And Jesus increased in wisdom and in stature and in favor with God and man. (Luke 2:49–52)

And as with Paul, this was determined before the world was created.

> In the sixth month the angel Gabriel was sent
> from God to a city of Galilee named Nazareth,
> to a virgin betrothed to a man whose name was
> Joseph, of the house of David. And the virgin's
> name was Mary. And he came to her and said,
> "Greetings, O favored one, the Lord is with you!"
> But she was greatly troubled at the saying, and
> tried to discern what sort of greeting this might
> be. And the angel said to her, "Do not be afraid,
> Mary, for you have found favor with God. And
> behold, you will conceive in your womb and bear
> a son, and you shall call his name Jesus. He will
> be great and will be called the Son of the Most
> High. And the Lord God will give to him the
> throne of his father David, and he will reign over
> the house of Jacob forever, and of his kingdom
> there will be no end."
>
> "**For nothing will be impossible with God.**"
> And Mary said, "**Behold, I am the servant of
> the Lord; let it be to me according to your
> word.**" And the angel departed from her. (Luke
> 1:26–33, 37–38)

So Peter, Paul, and Mary, all chosen by God and saved unto Christ, all walking in the works that God has prepared beforehand, to the counsel of His will. I submit for your consideration, why not the same for you and me?

Working Where God Has Placed You

> **Only let each person lead the life that the Lord
> has assigned to him, and to which God has**

called him. This is my rule in all the churches. Was anyone at the time of his call already circumcised? Let him not seek to remove the marks of circumcision. Was anyone at the time of his call uncircumcised? Let him not seek circumcision. For neither circumcision counts for anything nor uncircumcision, but keeping the commandments of God. **Each one should remain in the condition in which he was called.** Were you a bondservant when called? Do not be concerned about it. (But if you can gain your freedom, avail yourself of the opportunity.) For he who was called in the Lord as a bondservant is a freedman of the Lord. Likewise he who was free when called is a bondservant of Christ. You were bought with a price; do not become bondservants of men. **So, brothers, in whatever condition each was called, there let him remain with God.** (1 Cor. 7:17–24)

Paul tells us that God has placed each of us in roles that He has assigned, and through His Spirit, He now shares the wisdom for us to know that God uses us where He has placed us. So if you work in construction, stay in that role; if you work in sales, stay working in sales, but now be a light of the Gospel to all those around you so that "in whatever condition each was called there let him remain—**with God**." Of course, if God calls you to a specific role, such as teacher or pastor, by all means obey!

I will say to the north, Give up, and to the south, Do not withhold; bring my sons from afar and my daughters from the end of the earth, everyone who is called by my name, **whom I created for my glory**, whom I formed and made. (Isa. 43:6–7)

For we are created for His glory and have purpose to be used by God for His will to be done.

So for your further consideration, God places all men and women in time and in purpose for roles, and if you are a believer, then you have been called by God to believe, to see His glory, and to worship Him! Again, your blinders are now off, and you see Jesus for who He is! Not only is this humbling, this is also extremely exciting! This reality should cause you to think upon Christ continually, and that whatever you do, you do unto the Lord, for He has revealed and enabled you to see the glory of His grace toward you while you see the glory of His grace toward Himself—and with that, you should now know that His role for your life is secured within Him! So now when you read the Bible, it becomes your heart's desire to soak in the truth of the Gospel, for you put off the old man and are now anew!

You will not be Mary, that role has been filled, but you may raise children in the fear and knowledge of the Lord. You may not be Peter or Paul but can and should share the love of Christ with friends, family, and neighbors.

The learning is you are so loved by God that He came when you were still a sinner, and He cares for you, and He lives within you and you within Him, which I'll try to explain later on in the book; and Jesus sought you, and He bought you, paying the high price for your sins with His precious blood, His life, as atonement for your sins. And you are now FREE!

And know now that the blinders of the darkness of sin have been removed if you are in Christ, for you now can see the light of His glory and worship Him! AMEN! But humbly remember, it is all God's working within us and not we ourselves that saves us, and it is for His glory!

God Saves, but God Also Hardens

Sin has ugly side effects! Hell! Sin leads to pain and to death! Sin is godless!

THE SOVEREIGNTY OF GOD IN OUR DAILY LIVES

Leading into this section with a negative to illustrate the hardness of all men's hearts. For all that is sin is all that is against God.

Israel was God's chosen people for God to pour out His grace, mercy, love, and provision—for them as a people to be a light for all other nations to the glory of God, but alas, Israel (and in part Judah), as a nation, turned their hearts elsewhere. This is mostly seen in the previous covenant that God made with Israel, which Israel broke with God.

I cannot really give further explanation as to why God hardens hearts of some sinners and not of others, but to those he has hardened, God has a reason that is rarely known to us, and it always points to His holiness and His glory.

Continuing from Isaiah 6:

> And I heard the voice of the Lord saying, "Whom shall I send, and who will go for us?" Then I said, "Here I am! Send me." And he said, "Go, and say to this people: **'Keep on hearing, but do not understand; keep on seeing, but do not perceive.' Make the heart of this people dull, and their ears heavy, and blind their eyes; lest they see with their eyes, and hear with their ears, and understand with their hearts, and turn and be healed.**" (Isa. 6:8–10)

God sets a time of punishment upon Israel and Judah for their unrepentant sins again God and His Savior to come, but God, being full of compassion and mercy, will not make this an everlasting punishment.

> While I was speaking and praying, confessing my sin and the sin of my people Israel, and presenting my plea before the LORD my God for the holy hill of my God, while I was speaking in prayer, the man Gabriel, whom I had seen in the vision at the first, came to me in swift flight at the

time of the evening sacrifice. He made me understand, speaking with me and saying, "O Daniel, I have now come out to give you insight and understanding. At the beginning of your pleas for mercy a word went out, and I have come to tell it to you, for you are greatly loved. Therefore consider the word and understand the vision. Seventy weeks are decreed about your people and your holy city, to finish the transgression, to put an end to sin, and to atone for iniquity, to bring in everlasting righteousness, to seal both vision and prophet, and to anoint a most holy place. Know therefore and understand that from the going out of the word to restore and build Jerusalem to the coming of an anointed one, a prince, there shall be seven weeks. Then for sixty-two weeks it shall be built again with squares and moat, but in a troubled time. And after the sixty-two weeks, an anointed one shall be cut off and shall have nothing. And the people of the prince who is to come shall destroy the city and the sanctuary. Its end shall come with a flood, and to the end there shall be war. Desolations are decreed. And he shall make a strong covenant with many for one week, and for half of the week he shall put an end to sacrifice and offering. And on the wing of abominations shall come one who makes desolate, until the decreed end is poured out on the desolator." (Dan. 9:20–27)

Brothers, my heart's desire and prayer to God for them [Paul's fellow Jews] is that they may be saved. For I bear them witness that they have a zeal for God, but not according to knowledge. For, being ignorant of the righteousness of God, and seeking to establish their own, they did not submit to God's righteousness. For Christ is the end of the law for righteousness to everyone who believes. (Rom. 10:1–4)

But I ask, have they not heard? Indeed they have, for "Their voice has gone out to all the earth, and their words to the ends of the world." But I ask, did Israel not understand? First Moses says, "I will make you jealous of those who are not a nation; with a foolish nation I will make you angry." **Then Isaiah is so bold as to say, "I have been found by those who did not seek me; I have shown myself to those who did not ask for me."** But of Israel he says, "All day long I have held out my hands to a disobedient and contrary people." I ask, then, has God rejected his people? By no means! For I myself am an Israelite, a descendant of Abraham, a member of the tribe of Benjamin. God has not rejected his people whom he foreknew. Do you not know what the Scripture says of Elijah, how he appeals to God against Israel? "Lord, they have killed your prophets, they have demolished your altars, and I alone am left, and they seek my life." **But what is God's reply to him? "I have kept for myself seven thousand men who have not bowed the knee to Baal." So too at the present time there is a remnant, chosen by grace. But if it is by grace, it is no longer on the basis of works; otherwise grace would no longer be grace.** What then? Israel failed to obtain what it was seeking. **The elect obtained it,** but **the rest were hardened, as it is written, "God gave them a spirit of stupor, eyes that would not see and ears that would not hear, down to this very day."** And David says, "Let their table become a snare and a trap, a stumbling block and a retribution for them; let their eyes be darkened so that they cannot see, and bend their backs forever." (Rom. 10:18–11:10)

So I ask, did they stumble in order that they might fall? By no means! **Rather, through their trespass salvation has come to the Gentiles, so as to make Israel jealous**. Now if their trespass means riches for the world, and if their failure means riches for the Gentiles, how much more will their full inclusion mean! (Rom. 11:11–12)

God also hardens hearts

For the wrath of God is revealed from heaven against all ungodliness and unrighteousness of men, who by their unrighteousness suppress the truth. For what can be known about God is plain to them, because God has shown it to them. For his invisible attributes, namely, his eternal power and divine nature, have been clearly per-ceived, ever since the creation of the world, in the things that have been made. So they are without excuse. For although they knew God, they did not honor him as God or give thanks to him, but they became futile in their thinking, and their foolish hearts were darkened. Claiming to be wise, they became fools, and exchanged the glory of the immortal God for images resembling mortal man and birds and animals and creeping things. Therefore God gave them up in the lusts of their hearts to impurity, to the dishonoring of their bodies among themselves, because they exchanged the truth about God for a lie and wor-shiped and served the creature rather than the

Creator, who is blessed forever! Amen. (Rom. 1:18–25)

To the self-centered, self-consumed

And when he was alone, those around him with the twelve asked him about the parables. And he said to them, "To you has been given the secret of the kingdom of God, but for those outside everything is in parables, so that 'they may indeed see but not perceive, and may indeed hear but not understand, lest they should turn and be forgiven.'" (Mark 4:10–12)

Last days—the wrath of God to come

Therefore God sends them a strong delusion, so that they may believe what is false, in order that all may be condemned who did not believe the truth but had pleasure in unrighteousness. (2 Thess. 2:11–12)

More to be said regarding God's hardening hearts in the Last Days within chapter 18.

7

Prophesy of Jesus's Coming— Foreknowledge or Predestined?

And I was with you in weakness and in fear and much trembling, and my speech and my message were not in plausible words of wisdom, but in demonstration of the Spirit and of power, **so that <u>your faith might not rest in</u> the wisdom of men but in the power of God.** Yet among the mature we do impart wisdom, although it is not a wisdom of this age or of the rulers of this age, who are doomed to pass away. **But we impart a secret and hidden wisdom of God, <u>which God decreed before the ages</u> for our glory.** None of the rulers of this age understood this, for if they had, they would not have crucified the Lord of glory. But, as it is written, "What no eye has seen, nor ear heard, nor the heart of man imagined, what God has prepared for those who love him"—these things **God has revealed to us through the Spirit**. For the Spirit searches everything, even the depths of God. For who knows a person's thoughts except the spirit of that person, which is in him? So also no one comprehends the thoughts of God except the Spirit of God. Now we have received not the spirit of the world, but the Spirit who is from God, that we might understand the things freely given us by God. And we impart this in words not taught by human wisdom but taught by the Spirit, interpreting spiritual truths to those who are spiritual. **The natural person does not accept the things of the Spirit of God, for they are folly to him, and he is not able to understand them because they are spiritually discerned. The spiritual person judges all things, but is himself to be judged by no one. "For who has understood the mind of the Lord so as to instruct him?" But we have the mind of Christ.** (1 Cor. 2:3–16)

So I'm thinking about how to approach such a delicate subject as foreknowledge: A common misunderstanding is that God gives man "free will" and then looks down the corridors of time to see who will choose Christ—all prior to creation. And not to sound like a know-it-all, but I will offer the confidence of the Gospel as proof text to my brothers and sisters in Christ who say that faith is man's supplement to God's grace that results in salvation (the "last mile" or foresight of faith doctrine).

I've taken liberty to bold and underline a few words that I find key to grasp, to hold on to, and will also attempt to add further proof texts to show that foreknowledge is actually God actively working to set apart a person for salvation and not God passively coming to know how that man will act in the distant future, how he will choose when the Gospel is presented.

There are a few places within the New Testament that we find the words *foreknow*, *foreknew*, and *foreknowledge*, and many folks, including many fine contemporary Bible scholars, will hang their theology on this one word to say that God looks into the future to "see" who will "supply" faith or "come to Jesus on their own will," thus preserving man's free will or choice of believing in Jesus.

Two references are usually quoted in this regard:

> And we know that for those who love God all things work together for good, for those who are called according to his purpose. For those whom he foreknew he also predestined to be conformed to the image of his Son, in order that he might be the firstborn among many brothers. And those whom he predestined he also called, and those whom he called he also justified, and those whom he justified he also glorified. (Rom. 8:28–30)

> Peter, an apostle of Jesus Christ, To those who are elect exiles of the Dispersion in Pontus, Galatia, Cappadocia, Asia, and Bithynia, according to the foreknowledge of God the Father, in the sanctification of the Spirit, for obedience to Jesus Christ and for sprinkling with his blood. (1 Pet. 1:1–2)

A third reference for the word foreknew is used by Peter within his sermon of Acts, but many who hold the position that man supplies the deciding factor of personal choice to faith don't usually cite this sermon as a biblical reference in support of that understanding.

> Men of Israel, hear these words: Jesus of Nazareth, a man attested to you by God with mighty works and wonders and signs that God did through him in your midst, as you yourselves know—this Jesus, delivered up according to **the definite plan and foreknowledge of God**, <u>you crucified and killed by the hands of lawless men</u>. God raised him up, loosing the pangs of death, because it was not possible for him to be held by it. (Acts 2:22–24)

Notice the word order and strength of the sentence: this Jesus, delivered up, according, to the definite plan, and foreknowledge of God. Delivered, according, definite plan, and foreknowledge—of God. And then a flavor of Proverbs 16:9 on the back side of the verse: you crucified, you killed, and you are lawless men! Hard to see God's foreknowledge of choice in salvation, just man's sinfulness.

Okay, so putting aside the text of 1 Corinthians 2:3–16 for a moment, let us look just at the words of foreknowledge and then about how foreknowledge interplays within the earthly life of Jesus.

If God lets man make the ultimate decision based on man's free will to believe, if this is how being saved happens, I must ask: well, what about Jesus? As a man, did Jesus also have to supply his own faith and actions to foreknowledge too? For did God also have to look down the corridors of time to see how Jesus would respond? I hope most would say, "Of course not!" But please allow me to explain why I also say no, but in explaining, I hope to show that godly foreknowledge is not equal to man's free will in deciding.

This question makes me search to understand the meaning of the words *foreknow*, *foreknew*, and *foreknowledge*, and then by application, how those words are used within the context of the text.

Disclaimer number one, I am not a Hebrew or a Greek scholar, for I struggle with English, my one and only language, and as you read, you know it is obvious.

Disclaimer number two, my goal is not to discredit folks who hang their hat on foreknowledge as defined as God seeing the future and then responding to man within His planning; I am just saying I don't see the words saying that is so. You are brothers and sisters in Christ, although we disagree.

Biblical Foreknowledge Defined

I must turn to those smarter with the Hebrew and Greek than I to offer the definition, but in comparison, words have cultural as well as time applied relativity as to usage and application.

For example, growing up in the 1960s and 1970s, the word *cool* meant a condition of temperature, and it still does as I type this. But by application, my generation and even my kid's generation use this word to also mean agreement, liking, or of acceptance.

As an example, the standalone sentence, "That is cool." What does this mean?

Well, traditional English understanding should say that the "That," being the subject, reflects a condition of temperature; cool, being the predicate, that is somewhere between being cold and hot.

Now, what if I add context around the same sentence, what does cool mean?

Billy's dad says to Billy that "the store is out of chocolate ice cream, but they have strawberry. Would strawberry be acceptable?"

Billy's reply: "That is cool."

The word *that* now refers to not the ice cream but in the acceptance by Billy of strawberry ice cream over chocolate. My point is defining a word alone may not be the meaning of intent of the author; context is also valuable and important.

But remember, biblical truth is not culturally defined for the day, nor does the Word evolve to hold different meanings and applications over time. Therefore, we need to go back to understand the days of their writings of scripture and not to move the words of scripture forward and apply the meaning of those words to our day and age.[5]

Keep this in mind as you read the following quotes from folks more knowledgeable about Hebrew and Greek words and their usage than me.

With electronic publishing being pervasive these days, the following is a quote from the Monergism website, which then also quotes from John Murray and Robert Haldane, along with the comments from the author of the Monergism site:[6]

Quoted as to the whole block and raising the footnotes of Murray and Haldane for attribution, clarity, and rightful prominence. BOLD highlights are mine; italics are the respective authors.

---

[5] This would be a foundation for eisegesis: the interpretation of a text (as of the Bible) by reading into it one's own ideas.

[6] https://www.monergism.com/thethreshold/articles/onsite/foreknew.html

John Murray, from *The Epistle to the Romans*, Vol. I, pp. 316-318 defines Foreknew, as to the Hebrew and Greek having meaning of **cognition or awareness, or to acknowledge or to recognize**. In kind: "Before I formed you in the womb, I knew you," (Jeremiah 1:5)—I Corinthians 8:3, "But if one loves God, one is *known* by him," and also 2 Timothy 2:19, "the Lord knows those who are His." The Lord knows *about* all men but He only *knows* those "who love Him, who are called according to His purpose" (Romans 8:28)—*those who are His!*

Although the term "foreknew" is used seldom in the New Testament, it is altogether indefensible to ignore the meaning so frequently given to the word "know" in the usage of Scripture; "foreknow" merely adds the thought of "beforehand" to the word "know." Many times in Scripture "know" has a pregnant meaning which goes beyond that of mere cognition. It is used in a sense practically synonymous with "love," to set regard upon, to know with peculiar interest, delight, affection, and action (cf. Genesis 18:19; Exodus. 2:25; Psalm 1:6; 144:3; Jeremiah. 1:5; Amos 3:2; Hosea 13:5; Matthew 7:23; I Corinthians. 8:3; Galatians. 4:9; 2 Timothy 2:19; I John 3:1).* There is no reason why this import of the word "know" should not be applied to "foreknow" in this passage, as also in 11:2 where it also occurs in the same kind of construction and where the thought of election is patently present (cf. 11:5, 6). When this import is appreciated, then there is no reason for adding any qualifying notion and "whom He foreknew" is seen to contain within itself the differentiating element required. **It means "whom he set**

regard upon" or "whom he knew from eternity with distinguishing affection and delight" and is virtually equivalent to "whom he foreloved." This interpretation, furthermore, is in agreement with the efficient and determining action which is so conspicuous in every other link of the chain— it is God who predestinates, it is God who calls, it is God who justifies, and it is He who glorifies. Foresight of faith would be out of accord with the determinative action which is predicated of God in these other instances and would constitute a weakening of the total emphasis at the point where we should least expect it… **It is not the foresight of difference but the foreknowledge that makes difference to exist, not a foresight that recognizes existence but the foreknowledge that determines existence. It is a sovereign distinguishing love**. [*John Murray, *The Epistle to the Romans*, Vol. I, 316–318. Italics are his[7].]

Haldane, comparing Scripture with Scripture, clearly shows that the foreknowledge mentioned in Romans 8:29 cannot have reference to the foreseen faith, good works, or the sinner's response to God's call. **"Faith cannot be the cause of foreknowledge, because foreknowledge is before predestination, and faith is the effect of predestination. 'As many as were ordained to eternal life believed,' Acts 13:48.* Neither can it be meant of the foreknowledge of good works, because these are the effects of predestination. 'We are His workmanship, created in Christ Jesus unto good works; which God hath before ordained (or before prepared)**

[7] https://www.monergism.com/thethreshold/articles/onsite/foreknew.html

that we should walk in them'; Ephesians 2:10. **Neither can it be meant of foreknowledge of our concurrence with the external call, because our effectual calling depends not upon that concurrence, but upon God's purpose and grace, given us in Christ Jesus before the world began,** 2 Timothy. 1:9. **By this foreknowledge, then, is meant, as has been observed, the love of God towards those whom he predestinates to be saved through Jesus Christ. All the called of God are foreknown by Him, that is, they are the objects of His eternal love, and their calling comes from this free love. 'I have loved thee with an everlasting love; therefore with lovingkindness I have drawn thee'** Jeremiah. 31:3."[8] Murray, in rejecting the view that "foreknew" in Romans 8:29 refers to the foresight of faith, is certainly correct in stating that "It needs to be emphasized that the rejection of this interpretation is not dictated by a predestinarian interest. Even if it were granted that 'foreknew' means foresight of faith, the biblical doctrine of sovereign election is not thereby eliminated or disproven. For it is certainly true that God foresees faith;* he foresees all that comes to pass.* The question would then simply be: whence proceeds this faith which God foresees? And the only biblical answer is that the faith which God foresees is the faith he himself creates (cf. John 3:3–8; 6:44, 45, 65; Ephesians 2:8; Philippians 1:29; 2 Peter 1:2). Hence his eternal foresight of faith is preconditioned by his decree to generate this faith in those whom he foresees as believing, and we are thrown back upon the differentiation

---

[8] Robert Haldane, *Exposition of the Epistle to the Romans*, 397.

which proceeds from God's own eternal and sovereign election to faith and its consequents. The interest, therefore, is simply one of interpretation as it should be applied to this passage.* On exegetical grounds we shall have to reject the view that 'foreknew' refers to the foresight of faith."[9]

My takeaway: That biblical foreknowledge is **forelove** and akin to **cognition or awareness, or to acknowledge or to recognize. And summarized by Haldane:**

> By this foreknowledge, then, is meant, as has been observed, the love of God towards those whom he predestinates to be saved through Jesus Christ. All the called of God are foreknown by Him, that is, they are the objects of His eternal love, and their calling comes from this free love. "I have loved thee with an everlasting love; therefore with lovingkindness I have drawn thee" Jeremiah 31:3. (Ibid.)

Time for another weak metaphor to hopefully draw a contemporary parallel.

A young couple, within their hearts, plan to have a baby. Now I will not expound as that notion was from God—seeing that all babies are from God and that all names of those yet born, who have been called into salvation, have their names written within the Book of Life before the world began, and thus the predetermination of salvation of God is supported before birth—but I will just look at this from the perspective of Mom and Dad's point of view.

The child is conceived, and now Mom is carrying little Bobby or little Jamie. And about twelve or fifteen weeks go by, and it is time in today's wellness environment to have a sonogram.

---

[9]   Murray, *Romans*, 316.

Mom and Dad go the doctor's office, they have a sonogram done, the technician scans Mom's belly, she takes a picture, and they now know they will be having a baby boy! Excitement swells within the room! They now know before the child is born that the baby is Bobby—PAUSE—before Bobby is born. PAUSE. Now foreknown and foreloved by Mom and Dad. PAUSE. A boy!

Mom and Dad are experiencing foreknowledge…to **cognition or awareness, or to acknowledge or to recognize or to love.** Now twenty years later, Bobby asks Mom and Dad, "Did you know that I was going to be a boy in advance of my birth?" Mom and Dad can say yes, they foreknew that you were a boy, foreloved you, and prepared for you as such.

Foreknowledge is not causation of the child as to deciding what sex to be, and foreknowledge is not about God hoping before I was created that I will eventually believe in Him. Biblical foreknowledge is God setting His sovereign call of separation upon all he has predestined. He acknowledges, now as I read His word, that His foreknowledge is toward me, that I am His.

> For those whom he *foreknew* [set aside, loved], he also **predestined** to be **conformed** to the image of his Son, in order that he might be the first-born among many brothers. And those whom he **predestined** he also **called**, and those whom he **called** he also **justified**, and those whom he justified he also **glorified**. (Rom. 8:29–30)

Look at what follows HE foreknew: HE also predestined to be conformed; He also called; He also justified; and He also glorified. If just by context, foreknew cannot be man's "free will" determining when God's sovereignty will kick in. Thus God foreknew: declares, sets apart, purposes, finds, acknowledges, recognizes, loves me; and it is not I who declare, acknowledge, and recognize Him!

About Jesus's Coming, Foreknowledge or Prophecy?

Let us now look at Palm Sunday, under the consideration of foreknowledge (if defined as foresight of freewill) and prophecy.

> Now when they drew near to Jerusalem, to Bethpage and Bethany, at the Mount of Olives, Jesus sent two of his disciples and said to them, "Go into the village in front of you, and immediately as you enter it you will find a colt tied, on which no one has ever sat. Untie it and bring it. If anyone says to you, 'Why are you doing this?' say, 'The Lord has need of it and will send it back here immediately.'" And they went away and found a colt tied at a door outside in the street, and they untied it. And some of those standing there said to them, "What are you doing, untying the colt?" And they told them what Jesus had said, and they let them go. And they brought the colt to Jesus and threw their cloaks on it, and he sat on it. (Mark 11:1–7)

This amazes me! Jesus tells two of His disciples to go into the next village, and when they enter the village, they will see a colt, and not an ordinary colt mind you, but <u>one that has never been ridden on</u>. And Jesus instructs them to untie it and bring it back for Him, for Him to ride into Jerusalem. And then it gets even better! Jesus also tells them there will be people watching them take this colt. AND Jesus also tells the disciples that those folks will talk to them, and they will ask them what they are doing. And Jesus tells them what to say in reply. And to top it off, those folks in effect will say okay—"Makes sense, go ahead"—before it ever happened!

Foreknowledge or Predestination?

1. Preplanned? So did Jesus go to the city prior to His triumphal entry to preplan having the colt be there this day, and thus Jesus made arrangements with the owner of this colt hours, days, or weeks ago to have it ready in advance, and if by chance there would be people watching the disciples take this colt, thus telling them what to say and hope that would suffice?

2. Freewill Foreknowledge? Or did Jesus look into the future to see that there would be a colt in the village at this date and time, and that there would be people around watching and that Jesus saw this event unfold in foreknowledge and how it would play out and thus reported back to His disciples the outcome knowing it would work out?

3. Predestined? (This is what I see scripture declaring) Or that Jesus, being God, is working to accomplish the Father's will in all things leading to fulfilling all of the scriptures! Jesus thus works to the counsel of the will of God the Father, for whom God the Father has planned every detail of Jesus's earthly life, death, and resurrection before the foundation of the world, and that God planned that the colt, the "virgin' colt," would be there, that the crowd would watch the disciples unhitch the colt, and to even the planning the questioning of the disciples and their response!

All the while the disciples, and the people in the village, and the owner of the donkey were doing what they were doing as (to their own frame of living life unawares that) God had planned before the world was created. God is always using man and His actions to accomplish the counsel of His will. See Proverbs 16:9, and note:

> Rejoice greatly, O daughter of Zion! Shout aloud,
> O daughter of Jerusalem! Behold, your king is
> coming to you; righteous and having salvation is

he, humble and mounted on a donkey, on a colt,
the foal of a donkey. (Zech. 9:9)

(Are you still holding onto 2 Corinthians 2:7, "But we impart a secret and hidden wisdom of God, <u>which God decreed before the ages</u> for our glory"?)

So if God's foreknowledge were to relinquish to man's free will in choosing to believe and not in His separation in support of his calling, then all of man's choices in life would also be left to this definition of foreknowledge. The text and context within Romans 8, "For those whom he foreknew," does not say nor imply that this foreknowledge deals with man choosing to believe or just this one choice, but it belongs to God in His wisdom. God foreknows all things through His perfect wisdom, to the counsel of His will. And to those whom He elects, He foreknows (purposes) as to who they are (1 Pet. 1:1–2), and He is zealous to accomplish His will, and thy will be done! (Remember, to God, night is as bright as day!)

But one more time, if we say that foreknowledge means salvation is left to man to decide, then man making choices to believe also needs to apply to every choice man would make, for why limit this definition of foreknowledge to just the salvation decision within the text? To me this logic is inconsistent to application.

Stating this a different way…if God refrained from interfering with man's will to decide to believe in Jesus, then by the same principle, he will also refrain from interfering with all other decisions man would make…given this view of God's foreknowledge. I scratch my head not by the lack of words saying that foreknowledge means man choosing to believe, but it is only being applied to just one decision. (And what about all the new covenant scriptures we looked at in previous chapters?)

If foreknowledge was THE primary word and predestination, election, who are elect, predetermined plan, and glorification were subordinate to foreknowledge, then God's will has to also be predetermined in all things by the foreknowledge of God seeing man's response through all ages—if man's free will is to be preserved by foreknowledge…if defined not as an action of God but of God waiting on man. I hope that we both see this logic path would have to be "equally" applied to all of man's decisions if truly he had a free will, and now would give pause to reconsider, what does free will really mean? (See the chapter "Free Will = Willing Choices.")

But the text does not say man chooses. It says He (God) foreknew (knows us, all of us, that He has made His own). And again, one must add to the scripture any hint of man choosing as what God foreknew at best.

Time to take another look at a snippet of history, as recorded in John 9.

> As he passed by, he saw a man blind from birth. And his disciples asked him, "Rabbi, who sinned, this man or his parents, that he was born blind?" Jesus answered, "It was not that this man sinned, or his parents, but that the works of God might be displayed in him. We must work the works of him who sent me while it is day; night is coming, when no one can work. As long as I am in the world, I am the light of the world." Having said these things, he spit on the ground and made mud with the saliva. Then he anointed the man's eyes with the mud and said to him, "Go, wash in the pool of Siloam" (which means Sent). So he went and washed and came back seeing. (John 9:1–7)

"That the works of God might be displayed." "Work the works of Him who sent Me."

Foreknowledge of the blind man? Excuse the pun, but I cannot see how. Just as the blind man did not freely choose his blindness, he also did not choose his healing. It was a work of God alone.

So as God was planning creation, He set time and all events into view before the world began and every man and every woman ever to be created was ordained to be, and their times and seasons were ordered by His will. When all He "thought" would be precise to

Himself and His glory, He spoke into being, and all things became, according to His will! And now the time that I was born, and to the walk of life I am within, He marvelously planned before anything was created. Now through His Son, my Savior, and by the Holy Spirit, it has been "revealed to me" through being born again by His Spirit, that He willed my salvation, and I stand in awe praising His glory to behold!

These are my understandings. And every day is under His will, and my purpose is to seek Him continually, and He will direct (reveal) my path.

Or when God was planning creation, did he, through fore-knowledge, look at the beginning of His creation and fast-forward through to the end of time to see every event that would transpire? Is this how God acquired foreknowledge of man's free will to decide? Does God wait upon man to decide how to behave and what to choose? And then God writes His foreknowledge as prophecy of those events? Not at all what I see scripture saying.

Here is what C. S. Lewis thinks about predestination:

> "If God then is omniscient, he must have known what Abraham would do, without any experiment. Why then this needless torture?" But as St. Augustine points out, whatever God knew, Abraham at any rate did not know that his obedience would endure such a command until the event taught him: and the obedience which he did not know that he would choose, he cannot be said to have chosen. The reality of Abraham's obedience was the act itself; and what God knew in knowing that Abraham "would obey" was Abraham's actual obedience on that mountain top at that moment. To say that God "need not have tried the experiment" is to say that because

God knows, the thing known by God need not to exist.[10]

Question restated:

If within foreknowledge, would all the actions of the future be random to God (out of His control)? Did God set out to create all things, and then look throughout all time, first to see every event ever to "happen" from His plan of creation, thus he then "records" those events (prophecy) that were random to now be "predestined" to happen? This is not the scriptural view of God's sovereignty. Instead, God determines what will happen according to His intricate and personal plan; He declares it (prophecy), then, "The zeal of the LORD Almighty will accomplish this" (2 Kings 19:31; Isa. 9:7 and 37:32).

Need to revisit Romans 8:28–30 again:

> And we know that for those who love God all things work together for good, for those who are called according to his purpose. For those whom he foreknew he also predestined to be conformed to the image of his Son, in order that he might be the firstborn among many brothers. And those whom he predestined he also called, and those whom he called he also justified, and those whom he justified he also glorified.

He Foreknew, He Predestined, He Conformed, He Called, He Justified, and He Glorified Us—Those Who Love God

I am laboring over this with purpose. For it is so crucial to our faith to see that God is sovereign! And He is not passive but precisely active! In all things; behind every action; in every detail; and in every micron of time, space, and being.

---

[10] C. S. Lewis, *The Problem of Pain*, 101, https://www.desiringgod.org/articles/c-s-lewis-on-what-god-foreknows.

The text does not offer anything outside of God predestined, conformed, called, justified, and glorified. But in foreknew, it is His action—past tense. He predestined tells me He planned; He called tells me He initiated; He conformed indicates He changes me into the image of Christ; He justified indicates He accepted me in and though His Son; and He glorified is His future action toward me, through Christ!

I should stop here and be done, but let me go further. I need to. For the glory of God is at stake, as is my eternal security, for if man's will decides over God's will, then God is no longer sovereign; and if not sovereign, then my believing is left to my abilities, and I fail and struggle in everything in this life. I need Christ who has called me to securely hold me and hold me fast every day, and I cannot just rely on my grasping to hold on to Him. His grace towards me, if depending on my hands to control, I could decide tomorrow to let go and walk away. And if His grace doesn't hold me or even pursue after me to bring me back if I wander, then His grace toward me, left to my decision, to believe from within my "free will" loses life, and His Spirit within me would leave me, and if I lose Christ, woe to me! I am not smart enough, or strong enough, or good enough to save myself or to keep me saved!

So let us look at 1 Peter 1:1–2:

> To those who are elect exiles of the Dispersion in Pontus, Galatia, Cappadocia, Asia, and Bithynia, according to the foreknowledge of God the Father, in the sanctification of the Spirit, for obedience to Jesus Christ and for sprinkling with his blood: May grace and peace be multiplied to you.

To those who are elect. The action of being elect is to be called, chosen, and picked…like when we were younger and on the neighborhood basketball court when the team captain picks members for the basketball game from the street kids. We were all sizes and ages. Foreknowledge, if defined as man picking, would be like the captain of the team waiting passively to see which team each kid wants to play on, if any. This view of God does not fit the text of 1 Peter 1:1; instead, God picks the elect.

So I am back again to say that foreknowledge, foreknew, and foreknows, this knowledge comes from God's wisdom to know and control—all things. The donkey, the blind man's sight, Paul's conversion, and Peter's denial.

And what about God's hardening…of Israel, of perpetual sinners, and of the last days? Didn't God first tell Moses that He will harden Pharaoh's heart all the while Pharaoh hardened his heart as well? YES! And what about Nebuchadnezzar? How did God deal with him?

And when Joseph tells his brothers:

> "As for you, you meant evil against me, but God meant it for good, to bring it about that many people should be kept alive, as they are today. So do not fear; I will provide for you and your little ones." Thus he comforted them and spoke kindly to them. (Gen. 50:20–21)

It was God's plan, which He controlled from start to finish, for Joseph to be betrayed and sold by his brothers and to go through all those trials to eventually save his brothers and father.

And how does Paul's writing to the Ephesians about grace and faith fit in to foreknowledge?

> Blessed be the God and Father of our Lord Jesus Christ, **who has blessed us** in Christ with every spiritual blessing in the heavenly places, <u>even as **he chose us in him** before the foundation of the world</u>, that we should be holy and blameless before him. <u>In love **he predestined us for adoption to himself as sons through Jesus Christ,** according to the purpose of his will, to the praise of his glorious grace,</u> with **which he has blessed us** in the Beloved. <u>In him we have redemption through his blood, the forgiveness of our tres-</u>

> passes, according to the riches of his grace, which
> he lavished upon us, in all wisdom and insight
> **making known to us the mystery of his will**,
> according to his purpose, which he set forth in
> Christ as a plan for the fullness of time, to unite
> all things in him, things in heaven and things on
> earth. In him we have obtained an inheritance,
> **having been predestined according to the pur-
> pose of him who works all things according to
> the counsel of his will**, so that we who were the
> first to hope in Christ might **be to the praise of
> his glory**. In him you also, when you heard the
> word of truth, the gospel of your salvation, and
> believed in him, **were sealed with the promised
> Holy Spirit**, who is the guarantee of our inher-
> itance until we acquire possession of it, **to the
> praise of his glory**. (Eph. 1:3–14)

In the light of foreknowledge, my heart desires the understanding that man's will in making a choice to believe is not the determining factor in how salvation comes to man, even if God influences the
decision, as many would imply. But both by word definition and by
the context of the texts surrounding foreknowledge, coupled with
other texts regarding election, chosen, and predestination, all state
the contrary: it is all God. I don't exercise "free will" to be saved.

And then I need to compare other statements of predestination and election to see if foreknowledge, as being defined as man's
choices, is complimentary to other references.

> And **you were dead in the trespasses and sins** in
> which you once walked, following the course of
> this world, following the prince of the power of
> the air, the spirit that is now at work in the sons of
> disobedience—**among whom we all once lived
> in the passions of our flesh, carrying out the
> desires of the body and the mind, and were by**

nature children of wrath, like the rest of mankind. <u>But God, being rich in mercy, because of the great love with which he loved us</u>, even when we were dead in our trespasses, made us alive together with Christ—by grace you have been saved—and raised us up with him and seated us with him in the heavenly places in Christ Jesus, so that in the coming ages he might show the immeasurable riches of his grace in kindness toward us in Christ Jesus. **For by grace you have been saved through faith**. And this is not your own doing; it is the gift of God, not a result of works, so that no one may boast. For we are his workmanship, created in Christ Jesus for good works, which God prepared beforehand, that we should walk in them. (Eph. 2:1–10)

Paul's writings to the Ephesians testify to God's sovereignty and man's walking in sin and living in the passions of the flesh. Foreknowledge (in the human choices definition) takes away God's expression of His grace, takes away His love for us, and takes away His will of having a people He has chosen and describes a people who have chosen Him that He, in effect, comes to know by looking ahead in history (that He does not sovereignly control).

I have highlighted the text with underline and colors to show a few themes that may help some readers to see the sovereignty of God in believing a little more clearly. Take a moment in prayer and read the highlights as one thought each, then reread the verses again to put it all together. (As a former musician, I know that sometimes it helps to take a section at a time to work on, to get the part down right as the composer intended it to be played; seeing the pattern and themes helps get the music played rightly.)

I so value my brothers and sisters in Christ. My love for you all is godly in its nature. I have written much and have been repetitive in saying that God's foreknowledge is more akin to His predetermination than it is about His looking into the future to see what happens (man in control, rather than God). If you are reading this paragraph, you must know that I struggled in everything that I wrote beforehand, for I am praying to find a way to simplify, to make the point clearly that God is sovereign in our salvation calling.

But maybe the best way to close out this chapter is to let Paul instruct us again:

> Yet among the mature we do impart wisdom, although it is not a wisdom of this age or of the rulers of this age, who are doomed to pass away. **But we impart a secret and hidden wisdom of God, which God decreed before the ages for our glory.** None of the rulers of this age understood this, for if they had, they would not have crucified the Lord of glory. **But, as it is written, "What no eye has seen, nor ear heard, nor the heart of man imagined, what God has prepared for those who love him"**—these things **God has revealed to us through the Spirit**. For the Spirit searches everything, even the depths of God. For who knows a person's thoughts except the spirit of that person, which is in him? So also no one comprehends the thoughts of God except the Spirit of God. Now we have received not the spirit of the world, but the Spirit who is from God, that we might understand the things freely given us by God. And we impart this in words not taught by human wisdom but taught by the Spirit, interpreting spiritual truths to those who are spiritual. The natural person does not accept the things of the Spirit of God, for they are folly to him, and he is not able to understand them because they are spiritually discerned. The spiritual person judges all things, but is himself to be judged by no one. "For who has understood the

mind of the Lord so as to instruct him?" But we have the mind of Christ. (1 Cor. 2:3–16)

To God be the glory.

8

The Glory of God, the Glory of Jesus Christ—Righteousness, Holiness, Wisdom, and Grace

The heavens declare the glory of God, and the sky above proclaims his handiwork. (Psa. 19:1)

To the King of the ages, immortal, invisible, the only God, be honor and glory forever and ever. Amen. (1 Tim. 1:17)

Worthy are you, our Lord and God, to receive glory and honor and power, for you created all things, and by your will they existed and were created. (Rev. 4:11)

The glory of God, the glory of Jesus. Struggling now to type words fitting enough to leave the highest value of eminence of God and Jesus within you, but trusting that the Holy Spirit will bring this to heart more than any sentence I can muster.

In the same way, let your light shine before others, so that they may see your good works and give glory to your Father who is in heaven. (Matt. 5:16)

I could look up every biblical reference that declares God's glory, His righteousness, His name's sake, His holiness, and His worthiness; list them all below; and send to be published and call it done. But I want the opportunity to worship Him and praise Him for my kids and my kid's kids' sake. For them to know God the Father, God the Son, and God the Spirit, through my testimony, and for them to know and worship God too!

Here are two verses from the opening inner cover page:

> I will say to the north, Give up, and to the south, Do not withhold; bring my sons from afar and my daughters from the end of the earth, everyone who is called by my name, whom I created for my glory, whom I formed and made. (Isa. 43:6–7)

We were created for God's glory. Can I get an amen and a hallelujah!

> The LORD reigns, let the earth rejoice; let the many coastlands be glad! Clouds and thick darkness are all around him; righteousness and justice are the foundation of his throne. Fire goes before him and burns up his adversaries all around. His lightnings light up the world; the earth sees and trembles. The mountains melt like wax before the LORD, before the Lord of all the earth. The heavens proclaim his righteousness, and all the peoples see his glory. All worshipers of images are put to shame, who make their boast in worthless idols; worship him, all you gods! Zion hears and is glad, and the daughters of Judah rejoice, because of your judgments, O LORD. For you, O LORD, are most high over all the earth; you are exalted far above all gods. O you who love the LORD, hate evil! He preserves the lives of his saints; he delivers them from the hand of the wicked. Light

is sown for the righteous, and joy for the upright in heart. Rejoice in the LORD, O you righteous, and give thanks to his holy name. (Ps. 97)

Oh sing to the LORD a new song; sing to the LORD, all the earth! Sing to the LORD, bless his name; tell of his salvation from day to day. Declare his glory among the nations, his marvelous works among all the peoples! For great is the LORD, and greatly to be praised; he is to be feared above all gods. For all the gods of the peoples are worthless idols, but the LORD made the heavens. Splendor and majesty are before him; strength and beauty are in his sanctuary. Ascribe to the LORD, O families of the peoples, ascribe to the LORD glory and strength! Ascribe to the LORD the glory due his name; bring an offering, and come into his courts! Worship the LORD in the splendor of holiness; tremble before him, all the earth! Say among the nations, "The LORD reigns! Yes, the world is established; it shall never be moved; he will judge the peoples with equity." Let the heavens be glad, and let the earth rejoice; let the sea roar, and all that fills it; let the field exult, and everything in it! Then shall all the trees of the forest sing for joy before the LORD, for he comes, for he comes to judge the earth. He will judge the world in righteousness, and the peoples in his faithfulness. (Ps. 96)

Going back to my introduction, God's glory is primary, and the word *primary* does not seem to be strong enough to say here. I hold a few reserved words that I try hard not to use anywhere else except to God and for God! *Glory* is one of those words. *Exalted* is another. *Worship* and *praise* are right behind, and I even try hard to use *awesome* only for God, although sometimes I admit, I miss my mark. So Redeemer, or Savior, or Lord, or King, or to His attributes of merciful, the "glory of His grace," or long-suffering, of loving, of the summation of all attributes, pinnacle of my life!

But the point I want to share is God is the pinnacle. And to me, of life, for there is no one higher; no one greater; no one who is as God in wisdom, righteousness, holiness, value, worth, and treasure; and in return, God's grace, mercy, peace, joy, and love are eternally satisfying.

"What a mighty God we serve," for "He is worthy," "We exalt Him," and "How great Though art," although not scriptures, are great expression in song that uses scripture to worship and praise Him. All within this short chapter but maybe the most important chapter is to say that all glory and honor be to God!

It is now fitting to talk about prayer next!

9

The Power of Prayer

Think back about your childhood or your own children's childhood, whichever holds the best memories for you. I will write about looking back to my children as my best remembrance.

I remember when my kids first started to remember things and all the things they asked me. How things worked, when can they see Gram and Pappy? What are we going to do tomorrow, where was I going—to work—what did I do at work…so many questions and so many subjects that they were pondering. It makes me smile about their interest as well as to their knowing that Mom and Dad had control of their day, and with the questions, there was submission, for trust came easy for them at four and five years old.

In the same manner, God loves relationship with us. Prayer, as Jesus many times revealed, is highly valued by God.

Jesus Prayed

And He prayed a lot. For example, on Palm Sunday after Jesus's triumphal entry to Jerusalem, Jesus prayed publicly, and being fully God and fully man, His imminent death was troubling His human nature.

> "Now is my soul troubled. And what shall I say?
> 'Father, save me from this hour'? But for this
> purpose I have come to this hour. Father, glorify

your name." Then a voice came from heaven: "I have glorified it, and I will glorify it again." The crowd that stood there and heard it said that it had thundered. Others said, "An angel has spoken to him." Jesus answered, "This voice has come for your sake, not mine." (John 12:27–30)

Jesus openly prayed to the Father and yet confirmed the will of the Father to the glory of the Father. And God answered Jesus within seconds, aloud, not for Jesus's sake but for the crowd's sake. There is so much to glean from these four verses.

- Jesus's soul is troubled.
- Jesus contemplates asking the Father to remove Him from death on the cross.
- However, Jesus declares God's will and His purpose of the cross.
- Jesus prays to the Father.
- That the Father be glorified!
- God the Father replies as a voice out of heaven.
- Confirms Jesus's prayer that God the Father's name be glorified!
- And God will do it again, through the obedience of Jesus.
- Some within the crowd heard God the Father's answering Jesus's prayer as profound as thunder!
- Others said it was not God the Father but an angel.

Jesus offers the answer, His prayer for God to be glorified though Jesus's hour to come, and God confirms that Jesus's prayer is answered. The crowd, now hearing both the prayer and God's answer to Jesus's prayer, can testify to hearing God the Father! "I have glorified it [My Name], and I will glorify it again."

There is a month of sermons just within these verses, but focusing just on prayer, here is what I see.

- Jesus had a need.
- Jesus prayed to God the Father.
- Jesus wants God's will to be done.
- Jesus wants God to be glorified.
- God replies to Jesus.
- God confirms to Jesus that He has glorified His name.
- And He will do it again.

Let us look at the time of the transfiguration:

> Now about eight days after these sayings he took with him Peter and John and James and went up on the mountain to pray. And as he was praying, the appearance of his face was altered, and his clothing became dazzling white. And behold, two men were talking with him, Moses and Elijah, who appeared in glory and spoke of his departure, which he was about to accomplish at Jerusalem. Now Peter and those who were with him were heavy with sleep, but when they became fully awake they saw his glory and the two men who stood with him. And as the men were parting from him, Peter said to Jesus, "Master, it is good that we are here. Let us make three tents, one for you and one for Moses and one for Elijah"—not knowing what he said. As he was saying these things, a cloud came and overshadowed them, and they were afraid as they entered the cloud. And a voice came out of the cloud, saying, "This is my Son, my Chosen One; listen to him!" And when the voice had spoken, Jesus was found alone. And they kept silent and

told no one in those days anything of what they had seen. (Luke 9:28–36)

Again, Jesus prayed. And again, God responds. And again, and again, and again.

> But Jesus said, "They need not go away; you give them something to eat." They said to him, "We have only five loaves here and two fish." And he said, "Bring them here to me." Then he ordered the crowds to sit down on the grass, and taking the five loaves and the two fish, he looked up to heaven and said a blessing. Then he broke the loaves and gave them to the disciples, and the disciples gave them to the crowds. And they all ate and were satisfied. And they took up twelve baskets full of the broken pieces left over. (Matt. 14:16–20)

> And rising very early in the morning, while it was still dark, he departed and went out to a desolate place, and there he prayed. (Mark 1:35)

> Then Jesus went with them to a place called Gethsemane, and he said to his disciples, "Sit here, while I go over there and pray." And taking with him Peter and the two sons of Zebedee, he began to be sorrowful and troubled. Then he said to them, "My soul is very sorrowful, even to death; remain here, and watch with me." And going a little farther he fell on his face and prayed, saying, "My Father, if it be possible, let this cup pass from me; nevertheless, not as I will, but as you will." (Matt. 26:36–39)

And Jesus said, <u>"Father, forgive them, for they know not what they do</u>." (Luke 23:34)

Sidebar: My grandmother

I opened writing this book sharing my testimony, telling you about my quest to write this book about God's sovereignty in all things and in all ways. And I shared how hard it is to not write about one's self, but now as I begin to write on prayer and praying, I find it very hard not to share my witnessing my grandmother praying late one night with you.

I will try to keep it short, so I will say she was a tall 5'1", and that we have had many discussions as to what yardstick she was using

This fact is important because my grandmother lived to be 104, dying in the spring of 2007, and up until she was about ninety-three, she lived on her own after Granddad died in 1981. It was then at ninety-three that time had come for her to be with family on a more continued basis, so she sold her house and shared time living half a year with my mom and dad and the other half with my aunt and uncle.

Around the summer of 2004, my mom and dad had my grandmother during the summer months while my aunt and uncle went to see their kids and grandchildren in California and Oregon. And soon after they left for California, my mother took sick and had to have surgery on her heart unexpectedly. And this was a problem, for who was going to now watch Grandmother while Mom was in the hospital and then recovering?

God love my wife, for she didn't hesitate to say we will take her, so we took our first-floor living room that was private, for it was to the side of the house which had one way in and out, just past the steps for the second floor, and we made a curtain door for her privacy, and this became her bedroom. We moved out all the unimportant furniture and put in a bed for her, and with a sitting chair close by, and it was quaint. We had a full bath around the corner close by, and she moved very well now with the walker, for she was now about 101 years old, but as the Brits would say, still spry and chipper.

The company I worked for, to increase productivity as well as to cut costs, closed the local office, and thus I was now working from home. The good news is the commute was a breeze. The bad news is that I worked a lot more hours.

One night, around eleven thirty, I had just finished a conference call with folks from around the globe on a major global sales opportunity that we were working on, and I shut down the computer and was heading upstairs to bed. All the lights were off, except for a small beam of light pushing its way around the curtain door, and I thought it kind of late for my grandmother to still be awake.

So I paused to see if my grandmother needed something, or maybe something went wrong, and she needed help. As I went toward the curtain, I found her on her knees—praying! I don't think she realized I was at the curtain nor did I hear her pray, but I was so moved to see my tall 5'1" grandmother, kneeling beside her bed, with her walker beside her, submitting to our Lord in prayer.

I have such a sweet memory that has been burned into my heart that God has placed there for me to cherish, and I want my kids and their kids and their kid's kids to know that there is no age boundary, no time of day, and no physical limitation that thwarts having an intimate relationship with your Savior. Love the Lord with all your heart, and seek Him in prayer continually.

So pray.

> **Pray without ceasing**, give thanks in all circumstances; for this is the will of God in Christ Jesus for you. (1 Thess. 5:17–18)

> And he told them a parable to the effect that they ought always to pray and not lose heart. (Luke 18:1)

> **Praying at all times in the Spirit**, with all prayer and supplication. To that end, keep alert with all perseverance, making supplication for all the saints, and also for me, that words may be

given to me in opening my mouth boldly to proclaim the mystery of the gospel, for which I am an ambassador in chains, that I may declare it boldly, as I ought to speak. (Eph. 6:18–20)

Rejoice in the Lord always; again I will say, rejoice. Let your reasonableness be known to everyone. The Lord is at hand; **do not be anxious about anything, but in everything by prayer and supplication with thanksgiving let your requests be made known to God**. And the peace of God, which surpasses all understanding, will guard your hearts and your minds in Christ Jesus. Finally, brothers, whatever is true, whatever is honorable, whatever is just, whatever is pure, whatever is lovely, whatever is commendable, if there is any excellence, if there is anything worthy of praise, think about these things. What you have learned and received and heard and seen in me—practice these things, and the God of peace will be with you. (Phil. 4:4–9)

And to round out, Jesus gave wisdom and instruction as to what to pray for, how to pray, and where to pray within the Sermon on the Mount.

Pray then like this: "Our Father in heaven, hallowed be your name. Your kingdom come, your will be done, on earth as it is in heaven. Give us this day our daily bread, and forgive us our debts, as we also have forgiven our debtors. And lead us not into temptation, but deliver us from evil." (Matt. 6:9–13)

Acknowledge who God is; know that He is our Father. Understand that He is holy and that His will is being done, on earth as well as in heaven. God's kingdom is a physical kingdom prophetically coming to the earth. Also know that all that we have has been given to us by God, and that each day is sufficient unto itself. Seek repentance, the effort to see God's holiness and our sinfulness and to ask God to forgive us and to turn from sin, ask Him to lead us away from the temptations within us and to help us to also forgive others as He has forgiven us. And lastly, deliver us from evil, sin, the evil one. And ask God to help us to forgive others' sins toward us.

God is holy, God is our Father, God provides, God's kingdom will come to the earth, God's will be done, God forgives, God leads, and God delivers.

10

Praise, Glory, and Honor in God's Sovereignty Gives Comfort, Peace, Grace, Love, and Joy

But I say, **walk by the Spirit**, and you will not gratify the desires of the flesh. For the desires of the flesh are against the Spirit, and the desires of the Spirit are against the flesh, for these are opposed to each other, to keep you from doing the things you want to do. But if you are led by the Spirit, you are not under the law. Now the works of the flesh are evident: sexual immorality, impurity, sensuality, idolatry, sorcery, enmity, strife, jealousy, fits of anger, rivalries, dissensions, divisions, envy, drunkenness, orgies, and things like these. I warn you, as I warned you before, that those who do such things will not inherit the kingdom of God. **But the fruit of the Spirit is love, joy, peace, patience, kindness, goodness, faithfulness, gentleness, self-control; against such things there is no law.** And those who belong to Christ Jesus have crucified the flesh with its passions and desires. **If we live by the Spirit, let us also keep in step with the Spirit.**

Let us not become conceited, provoking one another, envying one another. (Gal. 5:16–26)

Look carefully then how you walk, not as unwise but as wise, **making the best use of the time**, because the days are evil. Therefore do not be foolish, but understand what the will of the Lord is. And do not get drunk with wine, for that is debauchery, but be filled with the Spirit, addressing one another in psalms and hymns and spiritual songs, singing **and making melody to the Lord with your heart, giving thanks always and for everything to God the Father in the name of our Lord Jesus Christ, submitting to one another out of reverence for Christ**. (Eph. 5:15–21)

And Paul and Barnabas spoke out boldly, saying, "It was necessary that the word of God be spoken first to you. Since you thrust it aside and judge yourselves unworthy of eternal life, behold, we are turning to the Gentiles. For so the Lord has commanded us, saying, 'I have made you a light for the Gentiles, that you may bring salvation to the ends of the earth.'" And when the Gentiles heard this, **they began rejoicing and glorifying the word of the Lord**, and <u>as many as were appointed to eternal life believed</u>. And the word of the Lord was spreading throughout the whole region. But the Jews incited the devout women of high standing and the leading men of the city, stirred up persecution against Paul and Barnabas, and drove them out of their district. But they shook off the dust from their feet against them and went to

Iconium. **And the disciples were filled with joy and with the Holy Spirit.** (Acts 13:46–52)

Just take a moment, a pause if you will, to ponder on all the stress of life that you might be experiencing right now. And in that pause, now reread this chapter from the beginning, and now look to see that God is in total control of every situation, even yours.

Sometimes when we need help to think, take a deep breath, maybe even a few deep breaths, to prepare to refocus. Now…let us head a bit deeper into the word to see that storms can be used for good; stress is not. Trials can build us up when we think they tear down.

So when the storms of life come…count it all joy! Really!

11

Enduring the Storms of Life

> Count it all joy, my brothers, when you meet trials of various kinds, for you know that the testing of your faith produces steadfastness. And let steadfastness have its full effect, that you may be perfect and complete, lacking in nothing. (Jas. 1:2–4)

And...

> Do not be conformed to this world, but be transformed by the renewal of your mind, that by testing you may discern what is the will of God, what is good and acceptable and perfect. (Rom. 12:2)

For...

> Blessed is the man who remains steadfast under trial, for when he has stood the test he will receive the crown of life, which God has promised to those who love him. (Jas. 1:12)

Count it all joy! So easy to say, so hard at times to do. When tough challenges come, and the word is not if but when, many times they come to test our faith to show us what we are made of.

And what I mean by that is God knows who are His, but He wants us to know that we are His, to confirm to ourselves. Trials and testing come to confirm to our own heart that we either belong to Christ or not. If we stand firm, being steadfast in our faith, now drinking bigger gulps of faith, our faith will weather the storm of trial or testing, if indeed we are in Christ and He in us. (See the later section on "The Always Filled Water Glass" for further support, page 208.)

Paul says to "renew your mind," particularly during the times of trials and testing. Dive deeply into the Bible, searching for God, getting to know Him through His grace and mercy for which God will give you discernment of His will. James says that if you remain steadfast, you will be blessed, confirming to yourself that you are saved, and you will receive the crown of life.

Know that as you study the word, as when you study anything, there is always application, and there will always be a test. And even if one never studies, the tests will still come. Better to study to be ready than to not study and fail.

> Beloved, do not be surprised at the fiery trial when it comes upon you to test you, as though something strange were happening to you. But rejoice insofar as you share Christ's sufferings, that you may also rejoice and be glad when his glory is revealed. If you are insulted for the name of Christ, you are blessed, because the Spirit of glory and of God rests upon you. But let none of you suffer as a murderer or a thief or an evil-doer or as a meddler. Yet if anyone suffers as a Christian, let him not be ashamed, but let him glorify God in that name. For it is time for judgment to begin at the household of God; and if it begins with us, what will be the outcome for those who do not obey the gospel of God? And "If the righteous is scarcely saved, what will become of the ungodly and the sinner?" Therefore let those

who suffer according to God's will entrust their souls to a faithful Creator while doing good. (1 Pet. 4:12–19)

Some tests come to directly glorify God. These tests come as testimonies of your faith in Christ. Peter wants us to know and not be surprised that if God has us within these types of trials, that we should submit to the glory of God by doing good!

For the time is coming when people will not endure sound teaching, but having itching ears they will accumulate for themselves teachers to suit their own passions, and will turn away from listening to the truth and wander off into myths. As for you, always be sober-minded, endure suffering, do the work of an evangelist, fulfill your ministry. (2 Tim. 4:3–5)

Remember Jesus Christ, risen from the dead, the offspring of David, as preached in my gospel, for which I am suffering, bound with chains as a criminal. But the word of God is not bound! Therefore I endure everything for the sake of the elect, that they also may obtain the salvation that is in Christ Jesus with eternal glory. The saying is trustworthy, for: If we have died with him, we will also live with him; if we endure, we will also reign with him; if we deny him, he also will deny us; if we are faithless, he remains faithful—for he cannot deny himself. (2 Tim. 2:8–13)

Faith

One little word, one big word. I would even say that faith is the hinge pin for a believer's relationship with Christ, our daily walk of faith, our running the race to finish, and our enduring the storms of life.

There are two types of faith: (1) one is temporal, (2) the other is God-breathed

Temporal faith is molded by conditions, formed by experiences, can house doubt inside it, and can also change over time.

Temporal faith says I will believe if (a) it makes sense, (b) I understand it, (c) it satisfies my desires, and (d) it is the current best option.

Temporal faith can include...

Planes trains and automobiles

Whereas we believe a plane can fly, that the pilot is well trained, that air traffic is monitored and controlled and that the passengers are civil and have self-control, and the weather will not bring down the plane.

We also can believe that there is a god, and even some Christians believe that we are right with God by the actions we do; the good things we do outweigh the bad, and that's all we need to do for God to let us into heaven. Many more examples could be given of temporal faith, but all suffer from earthly logic. Temporal faith covers a gamut of things and people. For we can also have faith in our country, believe in our leadership or company ethics, and then the country goes into turmoil, the leadership gets replaced, and the company goes out of business.

Without God's Spirit with us, this temporal faith will fail under pressure and testing. Without God's Spirit behind faith, which never fails, all others are as sinking sand.

So God gives faith, and God tests for faith. Not for Him to see what type of metal we are made of but for us to see of ourselves that our faith is God-breathed.

Count it all joy, my brothers, when you meet trials of various kinds, for you know that the testing of your faith produces steadfastness. And let steadfastness have its full effect, that you may be perfect and complete, lacking in nothing. (Jas. 1:2–4)

God-breathed faith

God-breathed faith is temporal faith's opposite. Faith is of God, is in God, thus supplied by God, is held by God, and the wisdom surrounding faith is given by God as assurance.

> Now faith is the assurance of things hoped for, the conviction of things not seen. For by it the people of old received their commendation. By faith we understand that the universe was created by the word of God, so that what is seen was not made out of things that are visible. (Heb. 11:1–3)

As we previously learned, by and through God's grace toward us, we are saved through faith, which is not temporal faith but is God's gifted faith in us. And as we also saw, God's gifted faith is toward God himself, and temporal faith covers a gamut of things and people.

> For by grace you have been saved through faith. And this is not your own doing; it is the gift of God. (Eph. 2:8)

> For everyone who has been born of God over-comes the world. And this is the victory that has overcome the world—our faith. (1 John 5:4)

> But the Scripture imprisoned everything under sin, so that the promise by faith in Jesus Christ might be given to those who believe. (Gal. 3:22)

So the miracle of salvation takes God's grace toward us, by His Spirit shining the light of the Gospel into a new heart of flesh now within us, and He supplies us with the wisdom of the Gospel of Christ, with the Spirit giving us the grace and faith of God.

> For by the grace given to me I say to everyone among you not to think of himself more highly than he ought to think, but to think with sober judgment, each according to the measure of faith that God has assigned. (Rom. 12:3)

> Until we all attain to the unity of the faith and of the knowledge of the Son of God, to mature manhood, to the measure of the stature of the fullness of Christ. (Eph. 4:13)

Time for another analogy...

The always filled water glass

Imagine that you have a large glass of water. And it is filled to the brim! In fact, imagine that every believer has the same sized glass of water, also filled to the brim.

Now imagine that the water represents faith. Each one of us has been given the same glass of water, and each glass is filled exactly the same. Now back to you...

And to that water, you drink from the glass, but you are taking sips. Two things to note: when you drink from the glass, the water is instantaneously replaced, never going down within the glass, for as you sip, the exact amount is being replaced, and thus you can have all the water you need and want.

Recapping. The glass is you (and me and other Christians with our own glasses). Water is faith. God gives and replenishes the water as you access the water/faith. You actually have access to the whole glass to drink from if you could take all of it in, but instead of taking big gulps of water, you are only are taking sips. God has given you the water, filled to the brim, at all times; all you need to do is to take bigger gulps.

So when we read within the Bible passage like, "Oh you of little faith,"

> Jesus immediately reached out his hand and took hold of him, saying to him, "<u>O you of little faith, why did you doubt?</u>" And when they got into the boat, the wind ceased. And those in the boat worshiped him, saying, "Truly you are the Son of God." (Matt. 14:31–33)

Or being "full of faith,"

> And what they said pleased the whole gathering, and they chose Stephen, <u>a man full of faith</u> and of the Holy Spirit, and Philip, and Prochorus, and Nicanor, and Timon, and Parmenas, and Nicolaus, a proselyte of Antioch. (Acts 6:5)

Know that it is not our faith that grows per se, but through godly wisdom, we have access to the faith we now possess in Christ Jesus through the Holy Spirit, who avails faith to us in full portion. But many times, we do not take bigger gulps, and sometimes we even take smaller sips in times of trials.

Not everyone accesses faith the same from day one

I appreciate the father of his son within Mark 9, who asks Jesus to heal his son. He comes to Jesus saying he believes, and yet he is having real trouble taking the bigger gulps of water that Jesus has at his ready:

> And Jesus said to him, "…All things are possible for one who believes." Immediately the father of the child cried out and said, "I believe; help my unbelief!" (Mark 9:23–24)

Applying my metaphor, "And the father replied, 'I am taking sips of faith. Help me to take bigger gulps of faith!'"

Therefore, Paul declares that grace and faith are a gift from God, and I say they are so closely related that you cannot have one without the other.

> And behold, there arose a great storm on the sea, so that the boat was being swamped by the waves; but he was asleep. And they went and woke him, saying, "Save us, Lord; we are perishing." And he said to them, "Why are you afraid, O you of little faith?" Then he rose and rebuked the winds and the sea, and there was a great calm. And the men marveled, saying, "What sort of man is this, that even winds and sea obey him?" (Matt. 8:24–27)

> And what they said pleased the whole gathering, and they chose Stephen, a man full of faith and of the Holy Spirit, and Philip, and Prochorus, and Nicanor, and Timon, and Parmenas, and Nicolaus, a proselyte of Antioch. (Acts 6:5)

> And I pray that the sharing of your faith may become effective for the full knowledge of every good thing that is in us for the sake of Christ. (Philem. 1:6)

> The Spirit and the Bride say, "Come." And let the one who hears say, "Come." And let the one who is thirsty come; let the one who desires take the water of life without price. (Rev. 22:17)

> But we ought always to give thanks to God for you, brothers beloved by the Lord, because God chose you as the firstfruits to be saved, through

sanctification by the Spirit and belief in the truth.
(2 Thess. 2:13)

Thomas's transition from temporal faith to God-breathed faith:

> Then he said to Thomas, "Put your finger here,
> and see my hands; and put out your hand, and
> place it in my side. Do not disbelieve, but believe."
> Thomas answered him, "My Lord and my God!"
> Jesus said to him, "Have you believed because
> you have seen me? Blessed are those who have
> not seen and yet have believed." (John 20:27–29)

When Life Hurts

Life is tough. Life can really stink. Sin, as we stated before, is ugly; it brings forth death and is judged to hell.

I am not talking the lures of sin's false attractiveness; I am talking the damnable consequences of sin and its separation from God.

There will be times that sin will have a season of effects on you. And in those times, it will be because of your behavior and actions. And then other times it will be because the actions of others, directly or indirectly.

Sin can also be seen in sicknesses, in tragedies, and in disasters. Because of the fall, the sin of Adam and Eve, sin affects all aspects of this world, and the pains of life bring tears and sorrows, if we let it.

For we know, there is good news! Actually, it is great news! Jesus has overcome the world!

> I have said these things to you, that in me you
> may have peace. In the world you will have tribu-
> lation. But take heart; I have overcome the world.
> (John 16:33)

> For everyone who has been born of God over-
> comes the world. And this is the victory that has

overcome the world—our faith. Who is it that
overcomes the world except the one who believes
that Jesus is the Son of God? (1 John 5:4–5)

So in the storms of life, in the pain of now, we can and should
have a calm, and through Christ we are able to endure, and it is built
around faith—the hope of and in Jesus Christ, who has overcome the
world, the sin, and the pain!

Rabbit Trail #3:

I sometimes wonder if the sin we still see and experience in this
world, after Jesus defeating sin and death at the cross, is still there for
a greater reason. Maybe the reason why sin is still allowed to be is that
God might use sin as a pointer to see the greater sin as being against
a holy, perfect, and righteous God. Until Jesus's return to judge the
world, sin still stands as evidence of the world's need of Christ, and
for our repentance and faith in Jesus.

Restated, as the world looks upon tragedy, many times people
will then rally together in support of each other. In times of tragedy,
we collect monies and develop programs and funding to beat a ter-
rible disease, a natural disaster, or a reaction to injustices which, to
the world, represent a sense of values. But when it comes to Jesus
and repentance, and loving God, loving Jesus, and loving people, the
worldly cause is silent!

I submit for consideration that if we as people would see sin as
God sees sin and that this is above sins' effects upon the world, the
focus would drive us to repentance and not to raising monies. Oh, if
we would only repent and seek after God as a society, how the pains
of sin would diminish! But this will only happen after Christ returns!

Sin's hold on the world is rooted deep. For the apostle Paul
again tells us so. With sin exposed in tragedy, man potentially can
see the effects of sin before himself, if not within himself. And if
God grants repentance, He may be given the bridge from sin unto
life through the pain the tragedy brings. So maybe, just maybe, God
uses these tragedies to show the world what sin looks like and maybe

to draw many into faith, through seeing the pain of sin. But alas, the world does not call it sin. But it is there in testimony for the day of judgment.

And yet for those who believe in Christ, it takes work on our part to recalibrate our focus to be on Christ and not on the sin, or its enticements, or its effects.

As believers in Christ, there is victory for cancer as a believer in Christ! There is victory when death calls us home! There is victory when sin changes this earthly life forever! Life does not stop, but the effects of sin will one day vanish, for we are in Christ, and He is in us!

Sin is painful, no doubt! But we live within the victory of the cross of Christ! God may heal us, and He may give us more days, or He may use the effects of sin to bring others to Christ. But ultimately the victory and prize is Christ![11]

> For I consider that the sufferings of this present time are not worth comparing with the glory that is to be revealed to us. For the creation waits with eager longing for the revealing of the sons of God. For the creation was subjected to futility, not willingly, but because of him who subjected it, in hope that the creation itself will be set free from its bondage to corruption and obtain the freedom of the glory of the children of God. (Rom. 8:18–21)

> When the perishable puts on the imperishable, and the mortal puts on immortality, then shall come to pass the saying that is written: "Death is swallowed up in victory. O death, where is your victory? O death, where is your sting?" The sting of death is sin, and the power of sin is the law. But thanks be to God, who gives us the victory through our Lord Jesus Christ. Therefore, my

---

[11] And remember, take big gulps from the water glass of faith instead of little sips.

beloved brothers, be steadfast, immovable, always abounding in the work of the Lord, knowing that in the Lord your labor is not in vain. (1 Cor. 15:54–58)

Therefore, since we have been justified by faith, we have peace with God through our Lord Jesus Christ. Through him we have also obtained access by faith into this grace in which we stand, and we rejoice in hope of the glory of God. Not only that, but we rejoice in our sufferings, knowing that suffering produces endurance, and endurance produces character, and character produces hope, and hope does not put us to shame, because God's love has been poured into our hearts through the Holy Spirit who has been given to us. For while we were still weak, at the right time Christ died for the ungodly. For one will scarcely die for a righteous person—though perhaps for a good person one would dare even to die—but God shows his love for us in that while we were still sinners, Christ died for us. (Rom. 5:1–8)

Faith Walking.

Likewise…

The Spirit helps us in our weakness. For we do not know what to pray for as we ought, but the Spirit himself intercedes for us with groanings too deep for words. And he who searches hearts knows what is the mind of the Spirit, because <u>the Spirit intercedes for the saints according to the will of God.</u> *And we know that for those who love*

God all things work together for good, for those who are called according to his purpose. (Rom. 8:26–28)

Not that I am speaking of being in need, for I have learned in whatever situation I am to be content. I know how to be brought low, and I know how to abound. In any and every circumstance, I have learned the secret of facing plenty and hunger, abundance and need. **I can do all things through him who strengthens me**. (Phil. 4:11–13)

And to be sure, Romans also declares that God even uses sin toward His glory and our benefit:

And we know that for those who love God all things work together for good, for those who are called according to his purpose. (Rom. 8:28)

I do not know many folks who open themselves up to God as David does. David has a way of not asking for just "things" but for the opportunity to grow closer to God, through humbly asking God to search his character and spirit:

Search me, O God, and know my heart! Try me and know my thoughts! And see if there be any grievous way in me, and lead me in the way everlasting! (Ps. 139:23–24)

Search me! Know my heart! Try me. Test me. Know my thoughts! See if there be any sin within me. Then lead me. In the way of everlasting! (Asking God to keep David from sinning against Him!)

What a prayer to ask of God! Asking God to test him, to be put under a trial. To show David his sins and weakness on David's asking. WITH the understanding that God will take hold and lead him into eternal life! Wow!

Faith walking takes the low road of humility, and David exemplifies this within this prayer and in Psalm 51.

Faith walking requires exuberant dependence, done in sincere humility, in realizing the need of Christ, in acknowledging sin within, in trust, by faith that God gives us in full strength, and seeing that only God is God, and we are not.

And in God's sovereignty, we are able to know that all things work together for good; all the pain, all the suffering we experience, is but temporary for those who are called according to His purpose.

To the Obedience of Faith

> For whatever does not proceed from faith is sin. (Rom. 14:23)

> Now to him who is able to strengthen you according to my gospel and the preaching of Jesus Christ, according to the revelation of the mystery that was kept secret for long ages but has now been disclosed and through the prophetic writings has been made known to all nations, according to the command of the eternal God, to bring about the obedience of faith—to the only wise God be glory forevermore through Jesus Christ! Amen. (Rom. 16:25–27)

God-breathed faith drives to the obedience of faith, for anything outside of faith is sin. Thus, we should walk by faith in the good works prepared beforehand for us.

216

12

Birds Fly, Flowers Will Bloom—
What, Me Worry?

Therefore I tell you, do not be anxious about your life, what you will eat or what you will drink, nor about your body, what you will put on. Is not life more than food, and the body more than clothing? Look at the birds of the air: they neither sow nor reap nor gather into barns, and yet your heavenly Father feeds them. **Are you not of more value than they**? And which of you by being anxious can add a single hour to his span of life? And why are you anxious about clothing? Consider the lilies of the field, how they grow: they neither toil nor spin, yet I tell you, even Solomon in all his glory was not arrayed like one of these. But if God so clothes the grass of the field, which today is alive and tomorrow is thrown into the oven, will he not much more clothe you, <u>O you of little faith? Therefore do not be anxious</u>, saying, "What shall we eat?" or "What shall we drink?" or "What shall we wear?" For the Gentiles seek after all these things, and your heavenly Father knows that you need them all. But seek first the kingdom of God and his righteousness, and all these things will be added to you. **Therefore <u>do</u>**

<u>not be anxious</u> about tomorrow, for tomorrow will be anxious for itself. Sufficient for the day is its own trouble. (Matt. 6:25–34)

Thus, seek the kingdom of God above everything else.

And Now a Word about Fear

Don't!

Okay, maybe a few more words. Not to be fearful or to worry or be afraid is easy to type but hard to apply. It is hard because as with Peter, our natural tendencies are to take our eyes off Jesus as we enter the stormy waters. For some reason, we run back to fear, uncertainty, and doubt when times get tough instead of running to the Word and the promises in which God in effect says, "I've got this."

> When I am afraid, I put my trust in you. In God, whose word I praise, in God I trust; I shall not be afraid. What can flesh do to me? (Ps. 56:3–4)

> And he awoke and rebuked the wind and said to the sea, "Peace! Be still!" And the wind ceased, and there was a great calm. He said to them, "Why are you so afraid? Have you still no faith?" And they were filled with great fear and said to one another, "Who then is this, that even the wind and the sea obey him?" (Mark 4:39–41)

And when trials and testings come, remember God strongly encourages an open-book testing approach.

13

The Sovereignty of God
in Our Daily Lives

Closing encouragement, understandings, and application.

> And because you are sons, God has sent the Spirit of his Son into our hearts, crying, "Abba! Father!" (Gal. 4:6)

Walking Faith

Good works that God has prepared

> Trust in the LORD with all your heart, and do not lean on your own understanding. (Prov. 3:5)

> For we are his workmanship, created in Christ Jesus for good works, which God prepared beforehand, that we should walk in them. (Eph. 2:10)

> **We exhorted each one of you and encouraged you and charged you to walk in a manner worthy of God, who calls you into his own kingdom and glory.** And **we also thank God constantly** for this, **that when you received the**

> **word of God**, which you heard from us, **you accepted it not as the word of men but as what it really is, the word of God, which is at work in you believers.** (1 Thess. 2:12–13)

If you will allow my hermeneutics to do some more puzzle fitting, now that we know it is God who is working in us and through us as Ephesians 2 declares, our awareness, our passion of love and gratitude to our Savior should bring forth trust…and fruit.

And as Paul tells us through his letter to the Thessalonians, and then to the church of Ephesus, we are to walk in a manner worthy of God, and to the calling of God toward us as being His possession, and to do it with all humility and gentleness, with patience, and with love for one another!

> I therefore, a prisoner for the Lord, **urge you to walk in a manner worthy of the calling to which you have been called, with all humility and gentleness, with patience, bearing with one another in love**, eager to maintain the unity of the Spirit in the bond of peace. There is one body and one Spirit—**just as you were called to the one hope that belongs to your call—** one Lord, one faith, one baptism, one God and Father of all, who is over all and through all and in all. [7] **But grace was given to each one of us according to the measure of Christ's gift.** (Eph. 4:1–7)

> And so, **from the day we heard, we have not ceased to pray for you, asking that you may be filled with the knowledge of his will in all spiritual wisdom and understanding**, so as to **walk in a manner worthy of the Lord**, fully pleasing to him: **bearing fruit in every good work and increasing in the knowledge of God**; being

strengthened with all power, according to his glorious might, for all endurance and patience with joy; **giving thanks to the Father, who has qualified you to share in the inheritance of the saints in light. He has delivered us from the domain of darkness and transferred us to the kingdom of his beloved Son,** in whom we have redemption, the forgiveness of sins. (Col. 1:9–14)

But I say, walk by the Spirit, and you will not gratify the desires of the flesh. For the desires of the flesh are against the Spirit, and the desires of the Spirit are against the flesh, for these are opposed to each other, to keep you from doing the things you want to do. **But if you are led by the Spirit**, you are not under the law. Now the works of the flesh are evident: sexual immorality, impurity, sensuality, idolatry, sorcery, enmity, strife, jealousy, fits of anger, rivalries, dissensions, divisions, envy, drunkenness, orgies, and things like these. <u>I warn you, as I warned you before, that those who do such things will not inherit the kingdom of God</u>. **But the fruit of the Spirit is love, joy, peace, patience, kindness, goodness, faithfulness, gentleness, self-control; against such things there is no law.** And those who belong to Christ Jesus have crucified the flesh with its passions and desires. **If we live by the Spirit, let us also keep in step with the Spirit. Let us not become conceited, provoking one another, envying one another.** (Gal. 5:16–26)

I am hoping the spirit of our Lord is now tenderizing your hearts to see how He moves within us to enable us to submit to His working in and through us. We Christians many times fail to seek to understand our walk of faith as we battle with self-desires each day. And notice that Paul many times shows us the pattern of life of those who have been saved, i.e., having the Holy Spirit residing within those who are called to faith in contrast with those who are not. Thus, he always reminds us to self-examine our hearts and motives daily.

This is why Paul declares, "Walk, work, live, and now seek":

> **If then you have been raised with Christ, seek the things that are above**, where Christ is, seated at the right hand of God. Set your minds on things that are above, not on things that are on earth. For you have died, and your life is hidden with Christ in God. When Christ who is your life appears, then you also will appear with him in glory. (Col. 3:1–4)

Set your mind on Christ, be determined, and be focused on Him! These are our actions; these become our desires for which we choose, to and for the glory of Christ!

In life we naturally react to circumstances, for this is part of our flesh. A voice is raised against us, we respond in rebellion, anger, or worse. When temptation sets before us, again we would naturally respond in the flesh and submit to it with truly little thought about sin.

But through the Spirit, we can, we could, we should, and we must walk in step with the Spirit. Restated again: now is the time for cognitive "willing choices" to take hold to live by the Spirit.

Paul is giving instruction that we now can truly see the glory of Christ, that our blinders now removed for the ways of the flesh to die, and the ways of the Spirit need to be fed and allowed to be nurtured.

The fruit of the Spirit becomes the self-evidence of feeding our spirit of life in Christ, through and in the Holy Spirit.

As we have learned that God gives faith, He grants repentance; He causes His laws to be written on our hearts; and He enables us to walk, to work, to live, and to seek. Our role is to also walk, also work, also to live, and also to seek.

Quoting again Proverbs 16:9,

> The heart of man plans his way, but the LORD establishes his steps.

But now know it is God within you and not you alone! The grace of His glory should be radiantly shining in you as the fruit of the Spirit manifests Himself within you!

In our birth and in our death

> For you formed my inward parts; you knitted me together in my mother's womb. I praise you, for I am fearfully and wonderfully made. Wonderful are your works; my soul knows it very well. My frame was not hidden from you, when I was being made in secret, intricately woven in the depths of the earth. Your eyes saw my unformed substance; in your book were written, every one of them, the days that were formed for me, when as yet there was none of them. (Ps. 139:13–16)

I treasure all of God's word, but Psalm 139 became one of my life verses early from the days of my spiritual birth.

I remember the first time I heard this chapter preached, for I teared up to see the glory of the Lord!

God's Working in the World around Us

God's allowing and/or preventing sin.

And what about "acts of God"?

In today's societies, almost every business contract has a provision regarding "acts of God" or force majeure. And it almost always refers to an "escape clause" from the obligations of the contract.

But what are acts of God to the world?

Merriam-Webster defines acts of God as

> An extraordinary interruption by a natural cause (such as a flood or earthquake) of the usual course of events that experience, prescience, or care cannot reasonably foresee or prevent.[12]

Merriam-Webster defines force majeure as

> 1: superior or irresistible force
>
> 2: an event or effect that cannot be reasonably anticipated or controlled
>
> In business circles, "force majeure" describes those uncontrollable events (such as war, labor stoppages, or extreme weather) that are not the fault of any party and that make it difficult or impossible to carry out normal business. A company may insert a force majeure clause into a contract to absolve itself from liability in the event it cannot fulfill the terms of a contract (or if attempting to do so will result in loss or damage of goods) for reasons beyond its control.[13]

We know that God controls the weather, for we remember the flood of Noah's days, that "he gives rain on the earth and sends waters

---

[12] https://www.merriam-webster.com/dictionary/acts%20of%20god
[13] https://www.merriam-webster.com/dictionary/force%20majeure

on the fields" (Job 5:10); He commands the winds and the water, and the shaking of the earth, and sends fire into judgment.

Calamities too?

> There were some present at that very time who told him about the Galileans whose blood Pilate had mingled with their sacrifices. And he answered them, "Do you think that these Galileans were worse sinners than all the other Galileans, because they suffered in this way? No, I tell you; but unless you repent, you will all likewise perish. Or those eighteen on whom the tower in Siloam fell and killed them: do you think that they were worse offenders than all the others who lived in Jerusalem? No, I tell you; but unless you repent, you will all likewise perish."
> (Luke 13:1–5)

Somehow, some way, all things are under the will of God, even the calamites in life.

How We Should Interact with God's Enablement

Pressure relief value

For me I have learned, and I am still learning to let go.

To know that God has all things under His control, both the macro things that surround me and the micro things within me, is like installing a pressure relief value.

> All things have been handed over to me by my Father, and no one knows the Son except the Father, and no one knows the Father except the Son and anyone to whom the Son chooses to

reveal him. Come to me, all who labor and are heavy laden, and I will give you rest. Take my yoke upon you, and learn from me, for I am gentle and lowly in heart, and you will find rest for your souls. For my yoke is easy, and my burden is light. (Matt. 11:27–30)

We should know that worry cannot change a circumstance, and fear cannot bring resolve, but that His Spirit supplies wisdom, peace, and joy, even when the temporal actives of life scream panic! We know that all things work together for good as God has ordained and that light shines out unto darkness and eliminates darkness instantaneously.

And the key is taking bigger gulps of faith when times seem tough. And to remember God's perspective is always better than our line of sight. Thus,

For we walk by faith, not by sight. (2 Cor. 5:7)

God knows us, even our thoughts and our prayers

Nathanael said to him, "How do you know me?" Jesus answered him, "Before Philip called you, when you were under the fig tree, I saw you." (John 1:48)

Notice that Nathanael was in awe. For he saw that Jesus knew him before Nathanael ever met Jesus.

Nathanael answered him, "Rabbi, you are the Son of God! You are the King of Israel!" (John 1:49)

Nathanael's response in seeing Jesus for who He is! He declares that Jesus is the Son of God! The King of Israel!

That should be our response as well! And with no holding back! Now let us take a glimpse into one of Daniel's prayers:

> While I was speaking and praying, confessing my sin and the sin of my people Israel, and presenting my plea before the LORD my God for the holy hill of my God, while I was speaking in prayer, the man Gabriel, whom I had seen in the vision at the first, came to me in swift flight at the time of the evening sacrifice. **He made me understand,** speaking with me and saying, "O Daniel, I have now come out **to give you insight and understanding.** At the beginning of your pleas for mercy a word went out, and I have come to tell it to you, for you are greatly loved. Therefore consider the word and understand the vision. (Dan. 9:20–23)

As Daniel began to pray, a word went out. God had set activities in motion at the first few words of Daniel's petition. And not after Daniel had finished but as he began to pray.

God knows our hearts. But more importantly, God molds our hearts. And He didn't have to wait until Daniel "signed off" his prayer before God "responds." God knows, and God's will drives Daniel, as he began to pray, from Daniel's own heart of confessing and pleading, that it was as God had purposed in Daniel. For God knew the needs of Daniel, as with Nathanael, and opened the understanding of both Daniel and Nathanael to see the glory of the Lord before them as they prayed!

> The plans of the heart belong to man, but the answer of the tongue is from the LORD. (Prov. 16:1)

In line with knowing Daniel's prayers, God also has a say in what we say. Think about this the next time you have the urge to say something that you should not even think, let alone say. It goes back to

> Know this, my beloved brothers: let every person be quick to hear, slow to speak, slow to anger; for the anger of man does not produce the righteousness of God. Therefore put away all filthiness and rampant wickedness and receive with meekness the implanted word, which is able to save your souls. (Jas. 1:19–21)

So to let God control our tongue as to what we say, knowing that God can either allow or prevent what proceeds from our hearts.

> The good person out of the good treasure of his heart produces good, and the evil person out of his evil treasure produces evil, for out of the abundance of the heart his mouth speaks. (Luke 6:45)

So…now that we can see and know,

> Let the words of my mouth and the meditation of my heart be acceptable in your sight, O LORD, my rock and my redeemer. (Ps. 19:14)

Ask God to help tame your tongue and your thoughts; to continue to create within you a new heart; and to no longer say things that hurt, or condemn, or lust after, or that are evil.

"Let the words of my mouth" is not self-ascribing but a prayer of acknowledgment saying to God, "Change me!" Knowing that, I now see my sin, asking God to change the words of my mouth and what I think about, so that it is acceptable to You O Lord, my rock and my Redeemer!

> For godly grief produces a repentance that leads
> to salvation without regret, whereas worldly grief
> produces death. (2 Cor. 7:10)

To the order of life we live.

As we saw by example, Peter, Paul, and Mary had unique and very visible roles that God had purposed for them to fulfill. And in the same manner, you and I also have been given unique roles in life to fulfill as well.

Before we were saved, and maybe even before you started reading this book, you may have never realized the calling God has given you in life, and it is with confidence I can declare to you that everything in your past, both the good and the bad, has been under the will of God.

So now that you know, you can rest. Rest in knowing that your future is in His hands, and now you can seek Him moment by moment, not in doubt or hesitation but in relationship. Resting in His Spirit, all you do can and should be for the glory of God!

> So, whether you eat or drink, or **whatever you
> do, do all to the glory of God**. (1 Cor. 10:31)

Adding to that:

> "And you shall **love the Lord your God with all
> your heart and with all your soul and with all
> your mind and with all your strength**." The second is this: "You shall love your neighbor as yourself." There is no other commandment greater than these. (Mark 12:30–31)

> Seek the LORD and his strength; seek his presence
> continually! (Ps. 105:4)

And in seeking add:

> **Humble yourselves**, therefore, under the mighty hand of God so that at the proper time he may exalt you, **casting all your anxieties on him**, because he cares for you. **Be sober-minded; be watchful.** Your adversary the devil prowls around like a roaring lion, seeking someone to devour. **Resist him**, firm in your faith, knowing that the same kinds of suffering are being experienced by your brotherhood throughout the world. And after you have suffered a little while, the God of all grace, who has called you to his eternal glory in Christ, will himself restore, confirm, strengthen, and establish you. (1 Pet. 5:6–10)

Humble yourself, casting all your anxieties on Him, be sober-minded, and resist the devil! Be firm (taking in big gulps of faith; see page 262).

> **Examine yourselves**, to see whether you are in the faith. **Test yourselves.** Or do you not realize this about yourselves, that Jesus Christ is in you?—unless indeed you fail to meet the test! (2 Cor. 13:5)

> **But grow in the grace and knowledge of our Lord and Savior Jesus Christ.** To him be the glory both now and to the day of eternity. Amen. (2 Pet. 3:18)

And take this to heart as if you were Timothy!

> For this reason I remind **you to fan into flame the gift of God**. (2 Tim. 1:6)

Thus,

> But I say, walk by the Spirit, and you will not gratify the desires of the flesh. (Gal. 5:16)

Now that we see salvation as an intimate relationship with Christ, our passion; our desire to follow, to live, and to die for, we are in love with our Savior. To serve and love Him, for His glory, is worthy of our response to:

> Be filled with the Spirit. (Eph. 5:18)

> So as to walk in a manner worthy of the Lord, fully pleasing to him: bearing fruit in every good work and increasing in the knowledge of God; being strengthened with all power, **according to his glorious might**, for all endurance and patience with joy; **giving thanks to the Father**, who has qualified you to share in the inheritance of the saints in light. (Col. 1:10–12)

Putting off the "old man":

> To **put off your old self**, which belongs to your former manner of life and is corrupt through deceitful desires. (Eph. 4:22)

And putting on the new man:

> And to be renewed in the spirit of your minds,[24] and **to put on the new self**, created after the likeness of God in true righteousness and holiness. (Eph. 4:23–24)

And

> Do not lie to one another, seeing that you have put off the old self with its practices and have put on the new self, which is being renewed in knowledge after the image of its creator. (Col. 3:9–10)

> But put on the Lord Jesus Christ, and make no provision for the flesh, to gratify its desires. (Rom. 13:14)

Proclaim the good news about Jesus.

> And I tell you, everyone who acknowledges me before men, the Son of Man also will acknowledge before the angels of God. (Luke 12:8)

And seek to grow, to fan the flame, to press on, and to even measure your progress:

> For this very reason, make every effort to supplement your faith with virtue, and virtue with knowledge, and knowledge with self-control, and self-control with steadfastness, and steadfastness with godliness, and godliness with brotherly affection, and brotherly affection with love. Therefore, brothers, be all the more diligent to confirm your calling and election, for if you practice these qualities you will never fall. (2 Pet. 1:5–7, 10)

> Not that I have already obtained this or am already perfect, but I press on **to make it my own**, because Christ Jesus has made me his own. (Phil. 3:12)

Not that I am speaking of being in need, for I have learned in whatever situation I am to be content. I know how to be brought low, and I know how to abound. In any and every circumstance, I have learned the secret of facing plenty and hunger, abundance and need. I can do all things through him who strengthens me. (Phil. 4:11–13)

And so...

Work out your own salvation with fear and trembling, for it is God who works in you, both to will and to work for his good pleasure. (Phil. 2:12–13)

14

The Body of Christ as the Church

We have spent most of our time looking at the sovereignty of God working within us by the call and gift of grace through faith in Christ Jesus in the process of God's salvation toward us. And now with the blinders toward the light of the glory of Christ being removed, we have been given the wisdom of God to salvation by the Holy Spirit, to see and to seek God's glory each day within us, as well as around us.

God has commissioned the "church" to be the gathering "place" of like-minded believers. The bigger church within some "denominational creeds" refers this to be all who name Jesus as Lord and Savior, which I agree with. My focus here is on God's sovereignty within our individual lives and to now see how this fits together from one to many, as the body of Christ—the church.

The Body of Christ and Individual Members

> For just as the body is one and has many members, and all the members of the body, though many, are one body, so it is with Christ. [13] For in one Spirit we were all baptized into one body—Jews or Greeks, slaves or free—and all were made to drink of one Spirit. 1 Corinthians 12:12-13

> But as it is, **God arranged the members** in the body, each one of them, **as he chose**. 1 Corinthians 12:18

> [27] Now you are the body of Christ and individually members of it. [28] And God has appointed in the church first apostles, second prophets, third teachers, then miracles, then gifts of healing, helping, administrating, and various kinds of tongues. [29] Are all apostles? Are all prophets? Are all teachers? Do all work miracles? [30] Do all possess gifts of healing? Do all speak with tongues? Do all interpret? [31] But earnestly desire the higher gifts. And I will show you a still more excellent way. 1 Corinthians 12:27-31

Paul shares that as a believer in Christ, we are in the body of Christ and thus a church member. And by a church member, this is not your action of reading the doctrinal statement of a local church you are involved with and signing a piece of paper agreeing to the doctrines. Paul is saying to all of us who have been called that we are part of the body of Christ and are members in Christ as the church, and each of us has a unique role within the body. Not a denomination, not a building, but a body of God-breathed believers.[14]

He speaks here of a local gathering and presents roles and administration and gifts to this gathering called the church. And in your and my call, go back to chapter 6 where we see God's calling of Peter, Paul, and Mary.

To each God has created and given a purpose for His glory, and Paul is also reinforcing the same within the church.

---

[14] Having common understandings—a doctrine of faith to like-mindedness of understanding what core scriptures teach—is very important to a local body of believers, but for this writing, this path will be viewed at a high level and not as a focal point. But know that having sound doctrine is of the utmost importance for a healthy local church to properly function as Christ has ordained.

God has appointed!

The body of Christ has many parts, and those parts serve the entire body as to their specific function to and for the glory of Christ! Thus, there is a togetherness required for God's working in you and through you by the counsel of His will for you AND the body of Christ. Membership is not joining; membership is the cognitive awareness of Christ within you and that we come together to...

Worship, Pray, Give, Teach, Preach, and Fellowship

And they devoted themselves to the apostles' teaching and the fellowship, to the breaking of bread and the prayers. And awe came upon every soul, and many wonders and signs were being done through the apostles. And all who believed were together and had all things in common. And they were selling their possessions and belongings and distributing the proceeds to all, as any had need. And day by day, attending the temple together and breaking bread in their homes, they received their food with glad and generous hearts, praising God and having favor with all the people. And the Lord added to their number day by day those who were being saved. (Acts 2:42–47)

Peter was kept in prison, but earnest prayer for him was made to God by the church. (Acts 12:5)

Until I come, devote yourself to the public reading of Scripture, to exhortation, to teaching. Do not neglect the gift you have, which was given you by prophecy when the council of elders laid their hands on you. Practice these things, immerse yourself in them, so that all may see your progress. Keep a close watch on yourself and on the teaching. Persist in this, for by so doing you will save both yourself and your hearers. (1 Tim. 4:13–16)

And the Lord's Supper, Baptisms

Jesus instructs, and some say, commands, two ordinances that the local church do

1. coming together to remember the life, death, and resurrection of Jesus through the taking of communion (the Lord's Supper); and
2. spreading the good news of salvation in and through Jesus Christ and baptizing them in the name of the Father, the Son, and the Holy Spirit.

Both activities, communion and baptism, are not a requirement to be saved but are a heartfelt response after being saved. There is no legalist intent that many churches impose, but if one is truly saved, one would desire to do as Jesus commands, remember Him in a special way, and identify with Him in believer's baptism.

Church Leadership

Then it seemed good to the **apostles and the elders**, with the whole church, **to choose men from among them** and send them to Antioch with Paul and Barnabas. **They sent** Judas called Barsabbas, and Silas, leading men among the brothers, with the following letter: The brothers, both the apostles and the elders, to the brothers who are of the Gentiles in Antioch and Syria and Cilicia, greetings. Since we have heard that some persons have gone out from us and troubled you with words, unsettling your minds, although we gave them no instructions, **it has seemed good to us, having come to one accord, to choose men and send them to you with our beloved Barnabas and Paul.** (Acts 15:22–25)

For an overseer, as God's steward, must be above reproach. He must not be arrogant or quick-tempered or a drunkard or violent or greedy for gain, but hospitable, a lover of good, self-controlled, upright, holy, and disciplined. He must hold firm to the trustworthy word as taught, so that he may be able to give instruction in sound doctrine and also to rebuke those who contradict it. For there are many who are insubordinate, empty talkers and deceivers, especially those of the circumcision party. They must be silenced, since they are upsetting whole families by teaching for shameful gain what they ought not to teach. One of the Cretans, a prophet of their own, said, "Cretans are always liars, evil beasts, lazy gluttons." (Tit. 1:7–12)

But as for you, **teach** what accords with sound doctrine. <u>Older men</u> are to **be sober-minded, dignified, self-controlled, sound in faith, in love, and in steadfastness.** <u>Older women likewise are to be reverent in behavior</u>, not slanderers or slaves to much wine. They are **to teach what is good,** and so <u>train the young women</u> to love their husbands and children, to be self-controlled, pure, working at home, kind, and submissive to their own husbands, that the word of God may not be reviled. Likewise, <u>urge the younger men to be self-controlled</u>. Show yourself in all respects to **be a model of good works, and in your teach-**

ing show integrity, dignity, and **sound speech** that cannot be condemned, so that an opponent may be put to shame, having nothing evil to say about us. Bondservants are to **be submissive** to their own masters [authority] in everything; they are to be well-pleasing, not argumentative, not pilfering, but showing all good faith, **so that in everything they may adorn the doctrine of God our Savior**. For the grace of God has appeared, bringing salvation for all people, training us to renounce ungodliness and worldly passions, and **to live self-controlled, upright, and godly lives in the present age, waiting for our blessed hope, the appearing of the glory of our great God and Savior Jesus Christ,** who gave himself for us to redeem us from all lawlessness and to purify for himself a people for his own possession who are zealous for good works. (Tit. 2:1–14)

Church Divisions and Church Discipline

I appeal to you, brothers, by the name of our Lord Jesus Christ, that all of you agree, and **that there be no divisions among you, but that you be united in the same mind and the same judgment**. For it has been reported to me by Chloe's people that there is quarreling among you, my brothers. What I mean is that each one of you says, "I follow Paul," or "I follow Apollos," or "I follow Cephas," or "I follow Christ." Is Christ divided? Was Paul crucified for you? Or were you baptized in the name of Paul? I thank God that I baptized none of you except Crispus and Gaius, so that no one may say that you were baptized in my name. (I did baptize also the household of Stephanas. Beyond that, I do not know whether

I baptized anyone else.) For Christ did not send me to baptize but to preach the gospel, and not with words of eloquent wisdom, lest the cross of Christ be emptied of its power. (1 Cor. 1:10–17)

It is actually reported that there is sexual immorality among you, and of a kind that is not tolerated even among pagans, for a man has his father's wife. And you are arrogant! Ought you not rather to mourn? Let him who has done this be removed from among you. For though absent in body, I am present in spirit; and as if present, I have already pronounced judgment on the one who did such a thing. When you are assembled in the name of the Lord Jesus and my spirit is present, with the power of our Lord Jesus, you are to deliver this man to Satan for the destruction of the flesh, so that his spirit may be saved in the day of the Lord. Your boasting is not good. Do you not know that a little leaven leavens the whole lump? Cleanse out the old leaven that you may be a new lump, as you really are unleavened. For Christ, our Passover lamb, has been sacrificed. Let us therefore celebrate the festival, not with the old leaven, the leaven of malice and evil, but with the unleavened bread of sincerity and truth. I wrote to you in my letter not to associate with sexually immoral people—not at all meaning the sexually immoral of this world, or the greedy and swindlers, or idolaters, since then you would need to go out of the world. But now I am writing to you not to associate with anyone who bears the name of brother if he is guilty of sexual immorality or greed, or is an idolater, reviler, drunkard, or swindler—not even to eat with such a one. For what have I to do with judging outsid-

THE SOVEREIGNTY OF GOD IN OUR DAILY LIVES

ers? Is it not those inside the church whom you are to judge? God judges those outside. "Purge the evil person from among you." (1 Cor. 5)

But in the following instructions I do not commend you, because when you come together it is not for the better but for the worse. For, in the first place, when you come together as a church, I hear that there are divisions among you. And I believe it in part, for there must be factions among you in order that those who are genuine among you may be recognized. When you come together, it is not the Lord's supper that you eat. For in eating, each one goes ahead with his own meal. One goes hungry, another gets drunk. What! Do you not have houses to eat and drink in? Or do you despise the church of God and humiliate those who have nothing? What shall I say to you? Shall I commend you in this? No, I will not. For I received from the Lord what I also delivered to you, that the Lord Jesus on the night when he was betrayed took bread, and when he had given thanks, he broke it, and said, "This is my body, which is for you. Do this in remembrance of me." In the same way also he took the cup, after supper, saying, "This cup is the new covenant in my blood. Do this, as often as you drink it, in remembrance of me." For as often as you eat this bread and drink the cup, you proclaim the Lord's death until he comes. Whoever, therefore, eats the bread or drinks the cup of the Lord in an unworthy manner will be guilty concerning the body and blood of the Lord. Let a person examine himself, then, and so eat of the bread and drink of the cup. For anyone who eats and drinks without discerning the body eats and drinks judgment on himself. That is why many of you are weak and ill, and some have died. But if we judged ourselves truly, we would not be judged. But when we are judged by the Lord, we are disciplined so that we may not be condemned along with the world. So then, my brothers, when you come together to eat, wait for one another—if anyone is hungry, let him eat at home—so that when you come together it will not be for judgment. About the other things I will give directions when I come. (1 Cor. 11:17–34)

If your brother sins against you, go and tell him his fault, between you and him alone. If he listens to you, you have gained your brother. But if he does not listen, take one or two others along with you, that every charge may be established by the evidence of two or three witnesses. If he refuses to listen to them, tell it to the church. And if he refuses to listen even to the church, let him be to you as a Gentile and a tax collector. Truly, I say to you, whatever you bind on earth shall be bound in heaven, and whatever you loose on earth shall be loosed in heaven. Again I say to you, if two of you agree on earth about anything they ask, it will be done for them by my Father in heaven. For where two or three are gathered in my name, there am I among them. (Matt. 18:15–20)

15

The Church: The Holy Spirit—Gifts

A Walk through 1 Corinthians 12

Before I begin, my goal is to always put God on display in all things, that His glory would be radiantly presented, and that we would see Him for who He is! As we walk the road of searching and now seeing His sovereignty in all things, the time has come to showcase His gifts of the Spirit and His fruit of the Spirit.

In this chapter, please take notice how Paul directs the gifts of the Spirit to the body of believers at Corinth, and just after his instruction regarding their gathering together for communion in chapter 11.

As we walk down this chapter together in a line-by-line fashion, look for the six Ws of Paul's instruction regarding the gifts of the Holy Spirit: who, what, where, when why, and how.

> Now concerning spiritual gifts, brothers, I do not want you to be uninformed. You know that when you were pagans you were led astray to mute idols, however you were led. Therefore I want you to understand that no one speaking in the Spirit of God ever says "Jesus is accursed!" and no one can say "Jesus is Lord" except in the Holy Spirit. (1 Cor. 12:1–3)

Notice the audience. A collective you—the church at Corinth. Also notice Paul is correcting their understandings regarding spiritual gifts and their former worship of idols and why they did what they did.

Now notice that Paul is saying in effect that if you are saved, you cannot, not should not, but you cannot say Jesus is accursed! So do not bring your former life as a pagan and how you worshipped pagan gods and mute (dumb) idols to God. For if you do, you are not in the Lord.

This makes me wonder, were there folks within the church speaking in tongues cursing God as they spoke?

So Paul opens this section with (1) I heard what happened, (2) I heard what was said, (3) that you were claiming to speak in the spirit of God, and (4) in that you cursed Jesus! No, no, no! No, this is not of God!

For Paul just finished correcting them about communion and the purposes thereof, and now he needed to give instruction to the gifts of the spirit of God.

It appears that they were fabricating the spiritual gifts, and Paul caught them and is now correcting them once again.

> Now there are varieties of gifts, but the same Spirit. (1 Cor. 12:4)

Moving to verse 4, we know that in being saved, the Holy Spirit does a lot within us. And we also know that He lives within us (1 Cor. 6:19). Praying in the spirit (Rom. 8:26) and living in the spirit (Rom. 8:5, 13).

Paul is schooling them about where these gifts originated from, and so it is not up to them to produce, because these many gifts come from God the Spirit.

> And there are varieties of service, but the same Lord. (1 Cor. 12:5)

And the same with service: varieties of gifts, varieties of service; same Spirit, same Lord. Service is a key point—need to apply the six Ws as we continue.

> And there are varieties of activities, but it is the
> same God who empowers them all in everyone.
> (1 Cor. 12:6)

Verses 4–6: varieties of gifts, varieties of service, and varieties of activities (gifts, service, and activities); same Spirit, same Lord, and same God.

- Gifts from same Spirit
- Service from same Lord
- <u>Activities from same God who empowers them all</u>
- IN EVERYONE, those "in the Holy Spirit" or my take those who are saved because of the Holy Spirit within them.
- Three: Spirit, Lord (Jesus), and God, who empowers them all in everyone (who believes).

Here is where I see an opportunity for misunderstandings. Depending on your theology regarding how one is saved, you can misunderstand the origin, the usage, and the type of gift one has, or as Paul states, receives.

If by man's free will I chose to believe, then the same mindset ascribes my choosing to receive a gift of the Spirit, then it is I and not God who calls God to deploy the gifts and not God who empowers by His "choice."

However, this is not what Paul is saying, for it is God who empowers, not we ourselves.

> To <u>each is given</u> the manifestation of the Spirit
> for the common good. (1 Cor. 12:7)

Manifestation is a big word for me, so I had to look it up in the dictionary to help me get a starting point of meaning.

Definition of *manifestation*:

1a: the act, process, or an instance of manifesting

1b(1): something that manifests or is manifest

1b(2): a perceptible, outward, or **visible expression**[15]

Going back to high school, I was told never to use the same word within the definition of the word to understand the meaning of the word, so I have to dismiss items 1a and 1b(1). I'll pick 1b(2) and say visible expression is what I'll apply here.

So to understand verse 7 better: "To each is given the *visible expression* of the Spirit for the common good."

Applying some Ws here:

- Who gives?
- Who receives?
- What is given?
- Who is it for?

Then Paul defines what they are:

> For to one is given through the Spirit the utterance of wisdom, and to another the utterance of knowledge according to the same Spirit. (1 Cor. 12:8)

Given through the Spirit:

- Spoken wisdom
- Spoken knowledge
- Faith

---

[15] Merriam-Webster Dictionary

- Healing
- Working of miracles
- Prophecy
- Distinguish between spirits
- Various kinds of tongues
- Interpretation of tongues

Does "One is given" read to only have one person in the local body? Or does Paul mean only one gift per person? And in either case, is it just one gift lasting forever? Or could one have many gifts but not at the same time? The answer is found in verse 11: given by the one and same Spirit, the Holy Spirit who apportions each one individually—as HE wills. So no amount, no time limit; whatever God wills to be—happens!

Notice that all are given. None are self-positioned to acquire. Also notice in absence that it is not a prerequisite or post-requisite for salvation. As HE (God the Spirit) WILLS.

> To another faith by the same Spirit, to another gifts of healing by the one Spirit, to another the working of miracles, to another prophecy, to another the ability to distinguish between spirits, to another various kinds of tongues, to another the interpretation of tongues. All these are <u>empowered by one and the same Spirit</u>, who apportions to each one individually as **he wills**. (1 Cor. 12:9–11)

Again, it is best I go to the dictionary to glean how to best understand *apportions*.

Definition of *apportion*:

> transitive verb
> : to divide and share out according to a plan.[16]

---

[16] Merriam-Webster Dictionary

Verse 11 restated: "The Spirit shares [empowers/enables] these gifts with each individual according to His plan and will."

> For just as the body is one and has many members,
> and all the members of the body, though many, are
> one body, so it is with Christ. (1 Cor. 12:12)

One body = many members is equal to many members of the body = one body. Applied to Christ.

Christ is the head of the body, whereas the body is one with many members.

> For in one Spirit we were all baptized into one
> body—Jews or Greeks, slaves or free—and all
> were made to drink of one Spirit. (1 Cor. 12:13)

A lot being said in this one sentence.

Let us take a look:

One Spirit—were all baptized into one body

One body—Jews, Greeks, slaves, and free are all equal, and all are in the one body (but with various roles and functions)

One Spirit baptized one body, i.e., the Spirit made the one body to drink of the one Spirit.

Thus, being IN the one Spirit, all are baptized into the body of Christ when we first believe, and that we were made to drink in the spirit individually to be one in the spirit.

Different water glass analogy.

As a believer, we know that God saves us by His grace through faith given to us, and that grace/faith is given to us 100 percent by God! And we saw that in our new faith, many times we only take sips instead of big gulps from "the always filled glass."

Now, to the gifts of the Spirit, there is another water glass analogy we can use to illustrate the gifts of the Spirit. This glass is labeled Gifts of the Spirit, and as it relates to gifts, it can be filled to any level, or it can be empty. There is no requirement as to level as being best in this analogy. The filling is by God; and the proportion, timing, duration, and benefit is given by God, for His glory.

This glass labeled Gifts does not represent salvation, nor does it represent having faith, or even baptism into the body of Christ, but is shared in example to show that it is proportioned by the owner, the Holy Spirit, and the glass is at the ready for use.

> All these are <u>empowered by one and the same</u>
> <u>Spirit</u>, who apportions to each one individually
> as **he wills.** (1 Cor. 12:11)

Recapping. The first water glass analogy I presented in chapter 11 is labeled Faith, and it is always filled by God to the brim and never diminishes with use by us.

We represent the glass; the water represents full faith given. The goal we have been charged to have is to be full of faith. Taking big gulps instead of little sips!

The second water glass analogy still represents us, and it is labeled Gifts of the Spirit. But now the filling of the glass is variable and can be empty or can be filled to various degrees by God.

As with faith, we have no charge to acquire or to fill the glass to any level, for it is God through the Holy Spirit that fills this glass as He is working through us. But we should use the fillings of the glass to its maximum potential at whatever level He gives.

So if God has given you the gift of teaching, then use the gift He has given you, and use it well.

But again, Paul says the gifts are not to be manufactured, or even to be coveted, but come as God wills. AND by God's EMPOWER-MENT! It is God working within us!

Remember what Paul declared?

> But by the grace of God I am what I am, and his
> grace toward me was not in vain. On the con-
> trary, I worked harder than any of them, though
> it was not I, but the grace of God that is with [in]
> me. (1 Cor. 15:10)

Collectively, the body of Christ has various roles and positions that God has designed, called, and thus implements, and God uses each one of us in the support of the body though worship to the Head, Jesus Christ.

> Now you are the body of Christ and individually members of it. And God has appointed in the church first apostles, second prophets, third teachers, then miracles, then gifts of healing, helping, administrating, and various kinds of tongues. Are all apostles? Are all prophets? Are all teachers? Do all work miracles? Do all possess gifts of healing? Do all speak with tongues? Do all interpret? But earnestly desire the higher gifts. And I will show you a still more excellent way. (1 Cor. 12:27–31)

To recap, God the Holy Spirit has a massive role in life and is equal to the Father and the Son in prominence.

> For the body does not consist of one member but of many. (1 Cor. 12:14)

This refers to group identification and reinforces one body = many members.

> If the foot should say, "Because I am not a hand, I do not belong to the body," that would not make it any less a part of the body. (1 Cor. 12:15)

Paul shares four examples regarding our individualism to the body of Christ to show the correlation to our spiritual connection in the body of Christ.

Being a foot is Paul's first example.

> And if the ear should say, "Because I am not an eye, I do not belong to the body," that would not make it any less a part of the body. (1 Cor. 12:16)

Being an ear the second example.

> If the whole body were an eye, where would be the sense of hearing? If the whole body were an ear, where would be the sense of smell? (1 Cor. 12:17)

And being an eye and nose the third and fourth example.

> But as it is, God arranged the members in the body, each one of them, **as he chose**. (1 Cor. 12:18)

For it is God who arranges the members within the body of Christ as He chose, not man choosing his position within the body of Christ. It is God choosing us and given us all a part of the body of Christ having roles: as the foot having a relationship to the hand, or the eye having a relationship to the ear or nose.

> If all were a single member, where would the body be? As it is, there are many parts, yet one body. The eye cannot say to the hand, "I have no need of you," nor again the head to the feet, "I have no need of you." On the contrary, the parts of the body that seem to be weaker are indispensable, and on those parts of the body that we think less honorable we bestow the greater honor, and our unpresentable parts are treated with greater modesty. (1 Cor. 12:19–23)

There are no insignificant parts in the physical body, for some of the "weaker" parts on the surface play an indispensable role in keeping the body healthy and functioning.

> Which our more presentable parts do not require. But God has so composed the body, giving greater honor to the part that lacked it, that there may be no division in the body, but that the members may have the same care for one another. (1 Cor. 12:24–25)

All are done by God. And may there be no comparison, thus division within the body, so that each part takes care of all the other members.

> If one member suffers, all suffer together; if one member is honored, all rejoice together. (1 Cor. 12:26)

United we stand, in suffering and in rejoicing. (And there is no falling!)

> Now you are the body of Christ and individually members of it. (1 Cor. 12:27)

Paul's declarative: You—plural—are the body of Christ, and then each one by name is to the members to it.

> And God has appointed in the church first apostles, second prophets, third teachers, then miracles, then gifts of healing, helping, administrating, and various kinds of tongues. (1 Cor. 12:28)

Now Paul goes into offices of the body of Christ, and take note who appoints.

- First, apostles
- Second, prophets
- Third, teachers
- Then miracles, one of the gifts
- Then gifts of healing, helping, administrating, and various kinds of tongues

It is God who appoints within the church.

> Are all apostles? Are all prophets? Are all teachers? Do all work miracles? (1 Cor. 12:29)

Then Paul asks a clarifying question. Are all

- apostles?
- prophets?
- teachers?
- miracle workers?

Do all possess gifts of healing? Do all speak with tongues? Do all interpret? (1 Cor. 12:30)

And he continues:

- Healers?
- Speaking in tongues?
- Interpreters?

Paul again clarifies not with the positive of who has these gifts and roles but asks in the negative to make a point. Do all possess...?

> But earnestly desire the higher gifts. And I will
> show you a still more excellent way. (1 Cor.
> 12:31)

Desire higher gifts, for which Paul will show a more excellent way. So to close out chapter 15, Paul talks about the body of Christ and the works of the Spirit, the Lord, and God—the Holy Spirit, Jesus, and the Father—and to show that the church has both a spiritual and physical aspect, having many members but being one body. And the physical church has needs as to roles of function, not roles of importance of one over another but roles to function as one. And Paul also declares that not everyone will have these roles.

But Paul opens the door to desire higher gifts and to desire strongly—with Paul's commitment to show a more excellent way!

Which goes into LOVE of 1 Corinthians 13.

Of the first nine gifts and eight roles/offices, we should have little aspiration of acquisition, for the distribution of these gifts and roles is by God's will through the Holy Spirit who imparts them. But to the HIGHER GIFTS, there is a declaration that Paul says to pursue: faith, hope, and love, with love being the greatest gift.

16

The Gifts of the Spirit Transforming into the Fruits of the Spirit

Is Love, Then, Both a Gift and a Fruit of the Spirit?

Great question. Let us dig in a bit deeper to find out.

> If I speak in the tongues of men and of angels, but have not love, I am a noisy gong or a clanging cymbal. And if I have prophetic powers, and understand all mysteries and all knowledge, and if I have all faith, so as to remove mountains, but have not love, I am nothing. If I give away all I have, and if I deliver up my body to be burned, but have not love, I gain nothing. Love is patient and kind; love does not envy or boast; it is not arrogant or rude. It does not insist on its own way; it is not irritable or resentful; it does not rejoice at wrongdoing, but rejoices with the truth. Love bears all things, believes all things, hopes all things, endures all things. Love never ends. As for prophecies, they will pass away; as for tongues, they will cease; as for knowledge, it will pass away. For we know in part and we prophesy in part, but when the perfect comes, the partial

will pass away. When I was a child, I spoke like a child, I thought like a child, I reasoned like a child. When I became a man, I gave up childish ways. For now we see in a mirror dimly, but then face to face. Now I know in part; then I shall know fully, even as I have been fully known. So now faith, hope, and love abide, these three; but the greatest of these is love. (1 Cor. 13)

Faith. Hope. Love. All three abide within those who believe. Love being the greatest!

Now look where Paul goes next:

- If I speak in tongues...
- If I have prophetic powers...
- If I understand all mysteries...
- If I have all knowledge...
- If I have ALL faith...
- If I give away all I have...
- If I deliver my body to be burned...

Paul just finished talking about the gifts of the Spirit that God gives at His discretion, and yet in rhetoric says that if you possess any one of these gifts and possess it to the utmost, but if you lack love, those gifts are worthless!

Let us go back to 1 Corinthians 11.

- Spoken wisdom
- Spoken knowledge
- Faith
- Healing
- Working of miracles
- Prophecy
- Distinguish between spirits
- Various kinds of tongues
- Interpretation of tongues

Paul now goes into usage of the gifts, particularly with the speaking in tongues and his desires for the congregation at Corinth. Notice that Paul leads with our action of pursuing, and then follows through with a desire. So the priority is chasing after love, capturing it, and with love intact, if God bestows a gift upon you, then the gift will bear fruit.

> Pursue love, and earnestly desire the spiritual gifts, especially that you may prophesy. For one who speaks in a tongue speaks not to men but to God; for no one understands him, but he utters mysteries in the Spirit. On the other hand, the one who prophesies speaks to people for their upbuilding and encouragement and consolation. The one who speaks in a tongue builds up himself, but the one who prophesies builds up the church. Now I want you all to speak in tongues, but even more to prophesy. The one who prophesies is greater than the one who speaks in tongues, unless someone interprets, so that the church may be built up. (1 Cor. 14:1–5)

Pursue LOVE. Desire spiritual gifts. Pursue is our action; desire here is an aspiration to have happen. As Paul continues, he writes almost to retract what he says earlier about gifts having differing values to the church and to God. The issue is that speaking in tongues has the opportunity to be counterfeited, in its speaking and in its purpose.

> But I say, **walk by the Spirit, and you will not gratify the desires of the flesh.** For the desires of the flesh are against the Spirit, and the desires of the Spirit are against the flesh, for these are opposed to each other, to keep you from doing the things you want to do. But **if you are led by the Spirit, you are not under the law**. Now the

works of the flesh are evident: sexual immorality, impurity, sensuality, idolatry, sorcery, enmity,
strife, jealousy, fits of anger, rivalries, dissensions, divisions, envy, drunkenness, orgies, and
things like these. I warn you, as I warned you
before, that those who do such things will not
inherit the kingdom of God. **But the fruit of the
Spirit is love, joy, peace, patience, kindness,
goodness, faithfulness, gentleness, self-control; against such things there is no law. And
those who belong to Christ Jesus have crucified the flesh with its passions and desires.**
If we **live by the Spirit**, let us also keep in step
with the Spirit. Let us not become conceited,
provoking one another, envying one another.
(Gal. 5:16–26)

Now, notice what Paul says the first fruit of the spirit is: LOVE.

Paul says, walk by the Spirit, be led by the Spirit, and later to
live by the Spirit. Walking, submitting, and living by the Spirit brings
the fruit of the Spirit.

Now notice that the gifts of the Spirit are bestowed at the will of
God. And we have the fruit of the Spirit—i.e., love, joy, and peace—
when we seek to walk and be led by the Spirit.

So God works both the gifts and the fruits of the Spirit; the gifts
come to those God has purposed, and the fruit of the Spirit comes
to all believers and, if I may say, at various strengths that we control,
so to speak.

In the fruit of the Spirit, more awareness becomes evident the
"closer" we walk by the spirit and we submit to be led by the Spirit.
The spirit of God evidences Himself through us that we have love,
joy, peace, patience, kindness, goodness, faithfulness, gentleness, and
self-control.

Paul then offers the contrast, if our attitudes and behaviors showcase the works of the flesh:

> Now the works of the flesh are evident: sexual immorality, impurity, sensuality, idolatry, sorcery, enmity, strife, jealousy, fits of anger, rivalries, dissensions, divisions, envy, drunkenness, orgies, and things like these. I warn you, as I warned you before, that those who do such things will not inherit the kingdom of God. (Gal. 5:19–21)

So love, is "more better," that possessing a gift of the Spirit and having the love of God within our heart should displace the love of flesh; thus, Paul reveals to us how.

> **And those who belong to Christ Jesus have crucified the flesh with its passions and desires.** If we live by the Spirit, let us also keep in step with the Spirit. Let us not become conceited, provoking one another, envying one another. (Gal. 5:24–26)

This is our service, to love the Lord with all of our heart and to love people, seeking to walk in the Spirit that testifies within us the commands and precepts of the Lord and to seek, submit, and live by the Spirit.

> Examine yourselves, to see whether you are in the faith. Test yourselves. Or do you not realize this about yourselves, that Jesus Christ is in you?— unless indeed you fail to meet the test! (2 Cor. 13:5)

17

Afterthoughts

The Days in Which I live

Up until this point, I have tried hard to limit my opinions and just focus on the word in an effort just to preach and teach the word. In this section though, I want to use all the learning of the previous chapters and apply them to life today. And in that, my opinions will be pronounced. Scripture is truth. Opinions are opinions. My prayer is that I stay faithful to scripture as I offer a life application view to contemporary events happening now and that I use the truth of God as I share my heart with you.

COVID-19 2020

Shut 'er down!

"Interesting times we live in" are on the lips of many folks today. As I type this, the world is in the throes of a flu pandemic, and this has put the whole world into disarray. We are told that this flu is different than all other flus because it does not have a vaccine or a prescribed treatment path to combat against it. And within folks whose immune systems are weak or who have a preexisting health issue, the mortality rate is high.

In the United States, everything nonessential has shut down for five months thus far. Now, opening and closing certain businesses based on daily health reports is the new norm. Social distancing and wearing face masks everywhere are expected and required. Schools are closed; folks who can work from home are doing so. And everyone is mandated to shelter at home, in the effort to curtail the spread of this virus. Government, education, health care, industry, retailing, transportation—the economy is limping along as the world hopes that distancing will be the answer to stop the spread of this flu. And the US government is printing and giving trillions of dollars to taxpayers and businesses in their effort to stop a global depression while "fighting the flu" through "hope" in science and a vaccine.

And all gatherings have been asked to stop. All sports, all movies, all conventions, all live entertainment, and even Hollywood entertainment have stopped producing new material for a season.

Even our churches

In the United States, God has gifted and granted us the liberties to gather, and we have tremendous freedoms to gather for worshipping God. And our churches, wanting to lead by example, are also moving from face-to-face gathering to video and computer broadcast services.

Interesting times we live in, indeed! So how does one respond? What does one think about?

What happens next?

Here is what I have been doing. I have been searching my own heart as God is prodding and seeing sin and confessing it before Him. And then I am praising God for who He is! For He is sovereign and in total control as we have seen and learned. For some, these are tumultuous times. For others, this might be a wake-up call to faith. But to those who are in Christ, we count each day as joy in our Lord and Savior (Jas. 1:2)

As believers in Christ, part of our prayer life should be to acknowledge the will of God. Jesus even tells us to pray for His return, "Thy kingdom come, on earth." And Jesus also tells us that no man knows the day or the hour of His return, but we can know the season, and we are to intently look for signs of His return.

Here is my take, as of mid-July 2020. I see God moving closer and closer to coming back for us Christians, as He said He would through Jesus Christ! Each day the news either gives a glimpse of entering the last days or evidence that the birth pangs are starting, if you will.

Sometimes scripture has both a near-term and a far-term application, and many times I see God casting a foreshadow within scripture to offer a "taste" of prophecy being fulfilled.

Like John 16:29–33:

> His disciples said, "Ah, now you are speaking plainly and not using figurative speech! Now we know that you know all things and do not need anyone to question you; this is why we believe that you came from God." …"Behold, the hour is coming, indeed it has come, when you will be scattered, each to his own home, and will leave me alone. Yet I am not alone, for the Father is with me. I have said these things to you, that in me you may have peace. In the world you will have tribulation. But take heart; I have overcome the world."

In reading this and now looking for applications, how does this fit, if at all? The churches in our town are not physically meeting at the moment. Interestingly, Jesus tells His disciples that they will all be scattered when Jesus's time came for Him to go to the cross, but also look at what else he says: "I have overcome the world." Makes me go hmmm.

That looks like a future-looking statement to the finished work of the cross stated as a done event. Thus, if I may take a second look, Jesus says, "The hour is coming"—future; "Indeed it has come"—present future to the time of the cross—"when you all will be scattered, each to his own home."

I see both a near and far-looking statement.

Continuing, "I have said these things to you, that in me you may have peace." A question comes to my mind: when the disciples scattered, did they have any peace? And my next question, John quotes Jesus saying, "In the world you will have tribulation." This certainly looks prophetically both near and far to me.

There are a lot of scriptures both within the Old Testament and within the New Testament that shows a near/far application, and I see this as one, maybe as a foreshadow of things to come. If not today, a marker to a future tomorrow.

And today within the world, there is unrest within Asia, the USA, and other places…would Matthew 24:12 have any value as describing what is happening today?

> And because lawlessness will be increased, the love of many will grow cold. (Matt. 24:12)

But then again, God says that our meeting together is vital to our spiritual health.

> Let us hold fast the confession of our hope without wavering, for he who promised is faithful. And let us consider how to stir up one another to love and good works, not neglecting to meet together, as is the habit of some, but encouraging one another, and all the more as you see the Day drawing near. (Heb. 10:23–25)

So many churches are struggling as to how to apply Romans 13, for does Paul write as to individuals or does he write to churches?

> Let every person be subject to the governing authorities. For there is no authority except from God, and those that exist have been instituted by God. Therefore whoever resists the authorities

resists what God has appointed, and those who
resist will incur judgment. (Rom. 13:1–2)

So what does one do?

Individually, know your line in the sand. Know where God's
commands are and where to draw the line to those commands. Jesus
says that there will be a falling away and that lawlessness will increase,
and love will grow cold.

Corporately, the need to assemble in times of confusion and
despair is valuable to the body of Christ. It is also valuable as a haven
for those for whom God is working within to draw them away from
their fear and from huddling at home in isolation.

Churches can and should be a rock in these uncertain times,
bringing God glory and a real instantaneous local mission to share
God's love that otherwise folks may have passed by. Having church
open during challenging times says, if stated biblically correct and
not politically correct, that Jesus is the rock in times of trouble and
that the Gospel is open, so come on in!

As governments and health care officials continue to modify
their standards of social distancing as their effort to curtail the spread
of this virus through the mandate of wearing of masks, and marking
floors and isles as to how to stay away from each other, and to curtail
gatherings of more than twenty-five people, the church can comply
with many of these precautions and still be open and be a haven of
rest where people come to worship, learn, teach, and pray and be a
light of the Gospel in a dark and getting darker world.

But again, Proverbs 16:9 declares, "**The heart of man plans his
way, but the Lord establishes his steps.**" What a wonderful God!
Seriously, consider that everything we say and do is always, somehow,
someway, within the will of God. What I hope we have seen by now
is that God, through Jesus Christ, His precious Son and our Lord
and Savior, has removed the blinders of sin from our eyes and given
us the ability to now have a cognitive awareness of Jesus 24-7. With
sixty minutes and sixty seconds line of sight to the glory of Christ!

But to be real, we sometimes forget that God has all things in
His hands. We sometimes plan and think and do things that if we

had a second thought about it and put it before God in that second thought, our choice of outcome would have been different.

But to God, our plan A and/or our plan B, C, or D is under God's plan A will, so what happened by our hand was what His will determined, all the while. Wow!

So what to do?

Be encouraged! Be prepared and get ready!

Always look within to self-examine for sin and repentance and then look for God's glory in all things! And trust in Him and Him alone!

Renew your mind within the Word of God and ask God to give you more wisdom and understandings.

And pray. Think upon Christ in all things and in all ways and pray with thanksgiving.

To Tell the Truth

Truth is becoming harder to identify within society. News, politicians, business, people—all are harder to identify what messaging is true and what is not, and traditional values are waning.

"Fake news," biases, and lies

I mention these attitudes of today not to take a position or give comment to the news or to take a political side to current events but to say that the world is full of lies and hate and false beliefs more today than ever. I see these worldly events coming into place to position the need for a type of unity, which I'm watching for within God's will.

> And because lawlessness will be increased, the
> love of many will grow cold. (Matt. 24:12)

> Now concerning the coming of our Lord Jesus
> Christ and our being gathered together to him,
> we ask you, brothers, not to be quickly shaken in
> mind or alarmed, either by a spirit or a spoken
> word, or a letter seeming to be from us, to the
> effect that the day of the Lord has come. Let no
> one deceive you in any way. For that day will not
> come, unless the rebellion comes first, and the
> man of lawlessness is revealed (2 Thess. 2:1–3)

Are we in an age of rebellion? Are we in an age where hearts are growing cold?

Are Things, All Events, All within the Will of God?

> Because God is sovereign and His will can never
> be frustrated, we can be sure that nothing hap-
> pens over which He is not in control. (R.C.
> Sproul, *The Will of God*)[17]

All things created

As we started and as we wind down to close, I am reminded to go back to Colossians 1:15–20:

> He is the image of the invisible God, the first-
> born of all creation. For by him all things were
> created, in heaven and on earth, visible and invis-
> ible, whether thrones or dominions or rulers or
> authorities—all things were created through him
> and for him. And he is before all things, and in
> him all things hold together. And he is the head
> of the body, the church. He is the beginning, the

---

[17] https://www.monergism.com/thethreshold/articles/onsite/wills_sproul.html.

firstborn from the dead, that in everything he might be preeminent. For in him all the fullness of God was pleased to dwell, and through him to reconcile to himself all things, whether on earth or in heaven, making peace by the blood of his cross.

Worthy are you, our Lord and God, to receive glory and honor and power, for you created all things, and by your will they existed and were created. (Rev. 4:11)

As an exclamation point to this book, v. 16 declares, "For by Him all things were created, in heaven and on earth, visible and invisible, whether thrones or dominions or rulers or authorities—all things were created through him and for him."

All things! Think of something—anything—Jesus created it. All things! Visible and invisible. Smiling? Yep, Jesus created it. Dirt? Yep! The good, the bad, and the ugly? Yep. All things!

Even sin? Even sin. Now, I am in no way shape or form advocating that God is sin! Scripture is quite clear that God is holy, righteous, pure, and cannot even look upon sin! But I am saying He provided for it, He defined it, He allowed it, and He uses it for His glory.

This resides within the deepest part of the theological pool to try and understand the "why." I am not smart enough to offer an answer as to the why, but I think I can offer a few thoughts as to how to look at sin through Scripture to see as part of the all things created, exists for, and to the glory of God!

The Scripture gives evidence of sin before creation (Satan's fall) to the garden of Eden, to the cross of Jesus, to the battle of Armageddon, and to the final rebellion at the end of the millennium and through judgment; sin is there.

For because of sin, Jesus was sent by God and came to save us from sin. He lived a perfect life, and yet He was crucified for sin by sinful people. He defeats sin and its penalty of death, and He defeats the father of lies. And now His glory is shining ever so brightly for those He came to save!

Sin is part of the all things created, the visible and invisible. It is a tough concept to grasp, for sure, but there will be a day when sin will be no more! Praise God!

By Him and for Him

Let us start this section through self-examination. That is natural, is it not? For we always start with self and then compare everything outwardly to self. So now that thought has been identified, let us change the frame of reference to Jesus.

You and I were created by Jesus. You and I belong to Jesus. All that Jesus created is for Jesus.

And Jesus is the head of all things!

May I have another AMEN!

The Topics I Did Not Cover in Detail

The many wills of God

Instead, I chose to focus on seeing the clarity between God's will and God's desire (see chapter 3).

Within the will of God, I could have gone to show through scripture that part of the "total" will of God is His "declarative will." And to be seen is His "permissive will." And then there is His "revealed will," which is the clearest to be recognized. And then there is God's "secretive will," which, conversely, is often difficult to identify.

But I chose to look at the will of God as a whole and not in part, and then made comparison to His desires, as scripture makes this distinction for us.

For as we will never find the word *Trinity* within the Bible—that of God the Father, God the Son, God the Holy Spirit, the Trinity—they are clearly declared all throughout the Bible. And it is so true to the various wills of God, yet at times it can be hard to discern without study and His Spirit leading us.

Knowing the will of God

This could be the foundation for another book, for this subject is as deep as it is wide.

Many of us will have times where we know what the will of God is for us, like Nehemiah knew to go back and rebuild the walls of Jerusalem at God's direction (Neh. 2:12; 7:5). And at other times we want to be precisely sure that our actions are in the will of God, as with Gideon and the laying of his fleece before God to make sure he understood that it was God directing him.

We know that every second in our past has been according to the will of God. This question, however, presupposes knowing the future will of God in the calling of life ahead. What we do know through Gideon, and the apostle Paul, and even by Jesus, is to seek the counsel of God in asking through prayer to the heart tugs "we may feel" of doing the will of God. Maybe if God allows, if He moves upon my heart to write another book to share through the word of "Doing the Will of God in Our Daily Lives," we can explore what is knowable and what is hopeful, to the walking the will of God each day.

The origin of sin

This is above my pay grade, as we used to say in my business professional life, when concepts or responsibilities or accountabilities were beyond us to explain or understand in detail. I see Scripture declaring that God has provided for sin to exist, but I have not been given the understanding to rightfully explain what this fully means.

My belief is that God defines everything, so I take this on faith that God planned for sin to be within His creation, for He defines what is good and what is evil, and He uses sin to the counsel of His will for ultimately His glory to be displayed.

When we open the Bible to Genesis, we see Satan has already fallen. We then see that Adam and Eve within their own heart, lusted into temptation, and from their heart, they coveted into the conception of sin to the birth of it. I can see the evidence of the first sin, but

I have not or cannot explain the why and the how from within their heart they sinned against God, who walked the earth with them in the cool of the morning.

I know that without sin, there would be no need for a Savior. But praise God that Jesus came to defeat sin, and He paid the price for me and for you who also believe!

And thus, Satan and his minions are always under God's permissive will

The book of Job offers a view into the workings of Satan to the counsel of the will of God and His permissions, and thus to say in recap that all things are under the control of our Lord and Savior, Jesus Christ, as we saw earlier within Colossians 1:15–20:

> He is the image of the invisible God, the first-born of all creation. For by him all things were created, in heaven and on earth, visible and invisible, whether thrones or dominions or rulers or authorities—all things were created through him and for him. And he is before all things, and in him all things hold together. And he is the head of the body, the church. He is the beginning, the firstborn from the dead, that in everything he might be preeminent. For in him all the fullness of God was pleased to dwell, and through him to reconcile to himself all things, whether on earth or in heaven, making peace by the blood of his cross.

Remember, that within Ephesians 1 and 2, we all were born as sinners, and thus God has saved all who believe, through the shining of the light to the glory of Christ within our hearts, and now we are children of the light and no longer children of darkness! Praise God!

The wheat and the tares

And/or the sheep and the goats. And/or the wheat and the chaff. And/or the wheat and the weeds. Seeing that this book is focused on God's sovereignty within individual believers, this subject would move away from that focus. However, this is a very important subject that needs study unto itself, for every Christian must always self-examine the mettle of your faith to make sure it is of and from God. Salvation is a works in progress from a human perspective, for "He who began a good work in *us* [you] will bring it to completion at the day of Jesus Christ."

Calvinism vs. Arminianism

Some folks, upon reading this book, will make a comparison of my writings between the labels of Calvinism and Arminianism. I purposely decided not to make the comparison or to open or introduce the subject, for this then would support those labels in either a propagating or in defensive way of one side or another.

By sticking with all scripture, it is my heart to proclaim the good news of the Gospel of Christ, and I choose to ignore the labels some may cling to and will let the Spirit of God deal with this within each heart as the Spirit sees fit.

And now…

What I Want to See Someday

In God's timing, I will one day see my Lord and Savior face-to-face, for He knows me with every wrinkle and every blemish and with every battle scar. But unlike Thomas, from doubt to faith, I want to see my Jesus, and I want a hug after gazing upon His glory. From faith to faith.

Oh, there is a lot more than one hug, for I long to see Him and hold Him and He hold me. It does not have to be long, but just long enough to enjoy the moment. And I want to see all the folks within the Bible. I want to see Paul and John and Peter and David, etc. And

I want to see my family who arrived there before me. I want to see my two grandsons, who never made it to birth; and of course my mom and dad; and the miracle of my father in-law, believing on his deathbed; and my grandparents and aunts and uncles that I saw God saving in the 1970s.

And I want to see Jesus's house. For "In my Father's house are many rooms. If it were not so, would I have told you that I go to prepare a place for you?" (John 14:2). I want to see the floors, the ceilings, like Ezekiel describes. It must be spectacular! And I want to see the new heaven and the new earth with the new Jerusalem coming down from heaven.

Naw...that's all good and that, but seeing my Lord and Savior and His glory is satisfying enough for me to ponder on for now! But I know that the glory of the Lord will be way beyond my scriptural understandings and imagination!

18

Come, Lord Jesus, Come!

God's Grace

From the revelation of the new covenant to now the revelation of Jesus's return, we have looked at a lot of scripture to see that God is active in all He has created.

That as we opened:

> The Lord of hosts has sworn: "As I have planned, so shall it be, and as I have purposed, so shall it stand." (Isa. 14:24)

For...

> Then the Lord said to me, "You have seen well, for I am watching over my word to perform it." (Jer. 1:12)

And I gave effort to show that all that He does includes His working within all He has created, even within you and me, according to the counsel of His will, for the glory of His grace.

> And I am sure of this, that he who began a good work in you will bring it to completion at the day of Jesus Christ. (Phil. 1:6)

God's Wrath

God is so loving and merciful, and His grace overflows to all of mankind. And yet the day is coming that Jesus will return to judge the sins of the world and to establish His earthly reign.

> Who is to judge the living and the dead, and by
> his appearing and his kingdom. (2 Tim. 4:1)

Sin. The wages for sin is death! And the wrath of God has been tempered while His will of grace works to fulfillment:

> For the wrath of God is revealed from heaven against all ungodliness and unrighteousness of men, who by their unrighteousness suppress the truth. For what can be known about God is plain to them, because God has shown it to them. For his invisible attributes, namely, his eternal power and divine nature, have been clearly perceived, ever since the creation of the world, in the things that have been made. So they are without excuse. For although they knew God, they did not honor him as God or give thanks to him, but they became futile in their thinking, and their foolish hearts were darkened. (Rom. 1:18–21)

For it is also time to restate that man's sin is the highest offense to God, as His glory is the most valuable attribute to Himself.

Christian circles in general and many churches specifically today so overlook or play down sin and its offenses to a holy and righteous God and focus only upon God's love and grace and mercy. I am not saying this is wrong, only incomplete.

Up until this point, of all the seventeen chapters prior to this were my effort to get us to this concluding chapter, that God is holy, He is righteous, and He is worthy of glory—thus sin must be dealt with.

And the praise and worship of all He has created is demanded, and now unrepentant sin outside the saving grace of Jesus Christ needs to be shown for what it is. The time will come that it will be avenged by a perfect, holy, and righteous God.

> We will all stand before the judgment seat of God; for it is written, "As I live, says the Lord, every knee shall bow to me, and every tongue shall confess to God." So then each of us will give an account of himself to God. (Rom. 14:10–12)

And…

> Therefore God has highly exalted him and bestowed on him the name that is above every name, so that at the name of Jesus every knee should bow, in heaven and on earth and under the earth, and every tongue confess that Jesus Christ is Lord, to the glory of God the Father. (Phil. 2:9–11)

As I hope you now will see, for those of us who are in Christ and Christ is within us, the wrath of God will pass over us because of the finished work of Jesus:

> For God has not destined us for wrath, but to obtain salvation through our Lord Jesus Christ, who died for us so that whether we are awake or asleep we might live with him. Therefore encourage one another and build one another up, just as you are doing. (1 Thess. 5:9–11)

> And to wait for his Son from heaven, whom he raised from the dead, Jesus who delivers us from the wrath to come. (1 Thess. 1:10)

Heavenly View from the Prophets

From the view that God is sovereign in our lives, and all things work together, and all sin must be accounted for, and Jesus will judge both the living and the dead, I find it hard to give the soon return of Jesus all the attention it rightfully deserves within this chapter to close out the book.

There are over six hundred references within the Old Testament and the New Testament that call attention to the second coming of Christ.

There are many great books that have been written that try to build a position as to how all the scriptures fit together for when Christ returns, and for now I will not go deep into an eschatological position to add to those books for this writing, but I say: be ready and pray that Jesus will come soon!

Remember that the sum of the word is truth; there are nuggets of building blocks toward Jesus's return in almost every book of the Bible.

But one nugget that speaks of Jesus's second coming I consider as a great starting point, and it is from Jesus Himself.

After preaching the Sermon on the Mount, His disciples asked Jesus two questions: When will you return and when will be the end of the age?

> As he sat on the Mount of Olives, the disciples
> came to him privately, saying, "Tell us, when will
> these things be, and what will be the sign of your
> coming and of the end of the age?" (Matt. 24:3)

Again, there is so much to share; however, I prefer not to go into the details within this writing but say that God has all He has created within His control, and to those who are called to dig deeper, pray, and start here within Matthew 24.

Then look back into the book of Daniel, specifically continue to Daniel 9:24–27 and chapter 12, as called out in Matthew 24:15 by Jesus. And then search and study into Isaiah, Micah, Zechariah and Malachi, the four Gospels, Thessalonians, Peter's letters, and of course the book of Revelation as starting points.

Then the questions you should be asking yourself are when does the Bible position the return of Jesus and then to rule on this earth as the disciples ask within Matthew 24:3, the millennial kingdom; and what happens with the church, with Israel and Judah, and with Satan and the Antichrist and his helper?

My position is that in each day our Lord allows is a day closer to Jesus's return, and I see scripture holding to a future time of the millennial kingdom—a position which in eschatology terms is called pre-millennialism.

As of this writing, no one knows the exact day and the hour, but Jesus testifies to look for the season of His return.

> From the fig tree learn its lesson: as soon as its branch becomes tender and puts out its leaves, you know that summer is near. So also, when you see all these things, you know that he is near, at the very gates. Truly, I say to you, this generation will not pass away until all these things take place. Heaven and earth will pass away, but my words will not pass away. (Matt. 24:32–35)

As to Jesus's return, Jesus tells us that He will return from the clouds:

> So when they had come together, they asked him, "Lord, will you at this time restore the kingdom to Israel?" He said to them, "It is not for you to know times or seasons that the Father has fixed by his own authority. But you will receive power when the Holy Spirit has come upon you, and you will be my witnesses in Jerusalem and in all Judea and Samaria, and to the end of the earth." And when he had said these things, as they were looking on, he was lifted up, and

a cloud took him out of their sight. And while they were gazing into heaven as he went, behold, two men stood by them in white robes, and said, "Men of Galilee, why do you stand looking into heaven? This Jesus, who was taken up from you into heaven, will come in the same way as you saw him go into heaven." (Acts 1:6–11)

Rabbit Trail # 4

Before I move forward, Luke, the author of Acts, records a third question about the future return and reign of Jesus.

So when they had come together, they asked him, "Lord, will you at this time restore the kingdom to Israel?" He said to them, "It is not for you to know times or seasons that the Father has fixed by his own authority." (Acts 1:6–7)

Add this to Matthew 24:3:

As he sat on the Mount of Olives, the disciples came to him privately, saying, "Tell us, when will these things be, and what will be the sign of your coming and of the end of the age?"

Three separate questions and three direct responses:
- The sign of your coming? Jesus then explains.
- Of the end of the age? Jesus then explains.
- Restore the kingdom to Israel? Jesus says it is not for you to know.

And when Jesus returns, He will come back as Judge and King, and in that,

> This is evidence of the righteous judgment of God, that you may be considered worthy of the kingdom of God, for which you are also suffering—since indeed God considers it just to repay with affliction those who afflict you, and to grant relief to you who are afflicted as well as to us, when the Lord Jesus is revealed from heaven with his mighty angels in flaming fire, inflicting vengeance on those who do not know God and on those who do not obey the gospel of our Lord Jesus. They will suffer the punishment of eternal destruction, away from the presence of the Lord and from the glory of his might, when he comes on that day to be glorified in his saints, and to be marveled at among all who have believed, because our testimony to you was believed. To this end we always pray for you, that our God may make you worthy of his calling and may fulfill every resolve for good and every work of faith by his power, so that the name of our Lord Jesus may be glorified in you, and you in him, according to the grace of our God and the Lord Jesus Christ. (2 Thess. 1:5–12)

> But, as it is written, "What no eye has seen, nor ear heard, nor the heart of man imagined, what God has prepared for those who love him." (1 Cor. 2:9)

Rabbit Trail #5: A Quick Eschatology Lesson

This chapter is becoming very hard not to go into deeper detail about the last days. For as I am reading this chapter over and over again as I write, and in reading I am trying to understand what I wrote from the reader's point of view, I find it might be difficult to grasp.

There is so much to say and know, for God tells us through His word in so many places about the events of those days, that it may help to offer some markers of the events that will happen. And this is not in any order on my part nor is it complete.

1. As of this writing, we are within the time of the Gentiles (Rom. 11:11–24). The age of God's grace as it is sometimes referred to.
2. Understand that there is a battle since Adam and Eve with sin and the devil, and Jesus defeated sin and the grave (1 Cor. 15:55–56).
3. And yet in victory, God has given grace to the world for a season and that Satan's time for total defeat is still on the clock (Rev. 20:7–10).
4. Also in view today is that God's love for Israel as a nation and as a people is running concurrently with their discipline and restoration through the age of grace into the time of the end (Dan. 9:16–27; Rom. 11)
5. Every day He brings to pass becomes part of the world's history of His will. God gives each day to fulfill, in part, both His hidden and revealed will toward His earthly kingdom (Matt. 6:10)!
6. Look back to the recent history of Israel, to the events of 1948, 1967, and 2017. Pray that God will do what He says he will do for Israel.
7. I understand through scripture that Satan both roams the world and accuses Christians of our sins before God in heaven, and that one day, God will tell the angel Michael, "Enough, kick Satan out of heaven" (Job 1:7; 1 Pet. 5:8; Rev. 12:10; Rev. 12:7–12).
8. In my eschatological studies, watch for a future peace treaty with Israel with key biblical markings (i.e., prophesy). There have been peace treaties in the past, but nothing that

stuck nor one that had an appeal that it was honest. The Bible declares that there will be a time when Israel will sign a treaty for seven years in their search for peace (Dan, 7; and it is within the duration of this specific treaty that "all hell breaks loose").

In Daniel and in Revelation, the terms *time, times,* and *half a time* appear. Time = one year. Times = two years. Half a time = days close to half a year. This is where I see seven years. (Daniel also writes toward seventy weeks of years, but for here, I will just mention it in passing, but this is also key to understand.)

And in my understandings of scripture, there will be TWO wraths in the last day events prior to God's judgment. I see the opening of the first six seals as being when Satan is kicked out of heaven and then the Antichrist and His helper appear on the scene. This is not directly from God, but is the wrath of Satan (Rev. 6)

And with the opening of the seventh seal, there is silence in heaven for about a half an hour, and now the wrath of God begins. Please note that through Jesus Christ, all Christians are protected from the wrath of God, for the atoning blood of Christ has paid for all our sins! Halleluiah! HOWEVER, not every Christian will be protected from the wrath of Satan (first six seals of the scroll being opened).

Last Days

So to my family and those who may read, the end of the Gentile age could be within your generation (Matt. 24:34), if not within mine, that the signs of Jesus's return take place. So know the word of God and know the signs of the days! I pray that you would ask for wisdom, and for understanding, and to know the will of God for your life, especially during this time. So know that God appoints some believers for persecution.

> Indeed, all who desire to live a godly life in Christ Jesus will be persecuted, while evil people and impostors will go on from bad to worse, deceiving and being deceived. (2 Tim. 3:12–13)

Others will be called to endure until death (Matt. 24:9).

And yet others will be given words to say when jailed for their faith in Jesus.

> Do not fear what you are about to suffer. Behold, the devil is about to throw some of you into prison, that you may be tested, and for ten days you will have tribulation. Be faithful unto death, and I will give you the crown of life. He who has an ear, let him hear what the Spirit says to the

churches. The one who conquers will not be hurt by the second death. (Rev. 2:10–11)

And others will be beheaded and martyred for faith in Jesus.

Some folks will be called before the government, and when that happens, God will give them the words to speak, for and in the name of Jesus! And they will go to court for their faith. And in this time there will be families who will break apart for the sake of their testimony in Jesus!

> But be on your guard. For they will deliver you over to councils, and you will be beaten in synagogues, and you will stand before governors and kings for my sake, to bear witness before them. And the gospel must first be proclaimed to all nations. And when they bring you to trial and deliver you over, do not be anxious beforehand what you are to say, but say whatever is given you in that hour, for it is not you who speak, but the Holy Spirit. And brother will deliver brother over to death, and the father his child, and children will rise against parents and have them put to death. And you will be hated by all for my name's sake. But the one who endures to the end will be saved. (Mark 13:9–13)

> But before all this they will lay their hands on you and persecute you, delivering you up to the synagogues and prisons, and you will be brought before kings and governors for my name's sake. This will be your opportunity to bear witness. Settle it therefore in your minds not to meditate beforehand how to answer, for I will give you a mouth and wisdom, which none of your adversaries will be able to withstand or contradict. You will be delivered up even by parents and brothers

and relatives and friends, and some of you they
will put to death. You will be hated by all for my
name's sake. But not a hair of your head will perish. By your endurance you will gain your lives.
(Luke 21:12–19)

And to those not in the faith, who reject the testimony of Jesus:

Therefore God sends them a strong delusion,
so that they may believe what is false. (2 Thess.
2:11)

They were scorched by the fierce heat, and they
cursed the name of God who had power over
these plagues. They did not repent and give him
glory. (Rev. 16:9)

For God has put it into their hearts to carry out
his purpose by being of one mind and handing
over their royal power to the beast, until the
words of God are fulfilled. (Rev. 17:17)

The invitation is always, always open!

The Spirit and the Bride say, "Come." And let
the one who hears say, "Come." And let the one
who is thirsty come; let the one who desires take
the water of life without price. (Rev. 22:17)

So...please read this next as one thought.

But the day of the Lord will come like a thief, and
then the heavens will pass away with a roar, and
the heavenly bodies will be burned up and dissolved, and the earth and the works that are done
on it will be exposed. Since all these things are

thus to be dissolved, what sort of people ought you to be in lives of holiness and godliness, waiting for and hastening the coming of the day of God, because of which the heavens will be set on fire and dissolved, and the heavenly bodies will melt as they burn! But according to his promise we are waiting for new heavens and a new earth in which righteousness dwells. (2 Pet. 3:10–13)

And my holy name I will make known in the midst of my people Israel, and I will not let my holy name be profaned anymore. And the nations shall know that I am the LORD, the Holy One in Israel. Behold, it is coming and it will be brought about, declares the Lord GOD. That is the day of which I have spoken. (Ezek. 39:7–8)

For behold, the day is coming, burning like an oven, when all the arrogant and all evildoers will be stubble. The day that is coming shall set them ablaze, says the LORD of hosts, so that it will leave them neither root nor branch. But for you who fear my name, the sun of righteousness shall rise with healing in its wings. You shall go out leaping like calves from the stall. And you shall tread down the wicked, for they will be ashes under the soles of your feet, on the day when I act, says the LORD of hosts. Remember the law of my servant Moses, the statutes and rules that I commanded him at Horeb for all Israel. Behold, I will send you Elijah the prophet before the great and awesome day of the LORD comes. And he will turn the hearts of fathers to their children and the hearts of children to their fathers, lest I come and strike the land with a decree of utter destruction. (Mal. 4)

But there is hope. The hope in a Savior for your sin and mine through the life, death, and resurrection of Jesus Christ.

For even in this time, when lawlessness increases and love grows cold, God still saves!

Conclusion

Again, to my son and daughter and her husband and to their children.

The disciples, while Jesus was sitting at the Mount of Olives after preaching, met with Jesus afterward and asked Him two questions:

> "Tell us, when will these things be, <u>and what will be the sign of your coming</u> and of <u>the end of the age?</u>" And Jesus answered them, "See that no one leads you astray. For many will come in my name, saying, 'I am the Christ,' and they will lead many astray. And you will hear of wars and rumors of wars. See that you are not alarmed, for this must take place, but the end is not yet. For nation will rise against nation, and kingdom against kingdom, and there will be famines and earthquakes in various places. All these are but the beginning of the birth pains. Then they will deliver you up to tribulation and put you to death, and you will be hated by all nations for my name's sake. And then many will fall away and betray one another and hate one another. And many false prophets will arise and lead many astray. And because lawlessness will be increased, the love of many will grow cold. But the one who endures to the end will be saved. And this gospel of the kingdom

will be proclaimed throughout the whole world
as a testimony to all nations, and then the end
will come." (Matt. 24:3–14)

If Jesus tarries from returning into another generation, I want
to pass along to you my desire for you to pray as I have, that God
would always be glorified in your prayers and in the life He has given
you and that you would ask God to give you eyes that can see and
ears that can hear in praying daily for wisdom, with understanding.

And pray for His return and be cognitively aware in your prayers
by studying His Word, as the world's godlessness increases.

And teach them to your children, to instruct them in the truth
and knowledge of our Lord and Savior, Jesus Christ. And I pray that
this behavior turns into your desire, becoming etched within your
heart by God. I want you to know that God's Spirit is in you, and this
is your evidence, that your love of Jesus is becoming more focused as
the world rebels against Him more each day!

Stand firm in your faith that God has given you, and as Paul
instructs Timothy, I leave instruction for you to also "fan the flame
of your faith."

The days are coming when Jesus will return, and what a wonderful day that will be. If God gives us a day or many decades, be
always at the ready, and do the work of a missionary, sharing the love
of Christ to a lost and dying world wherever and whenever you can.

Rejoice always, pray without ceasing, give thanks
in all circumstances; for this is the will of God in
Christ Jesus for you. Do not quench the Spirit.
Do not despise prophecies, but test everything;
hold fast what is good. Abstain from every form
of evil. (1 Thess. 5:16–22)

Father, thank You for all that You are. For Your glory! For Your
holiness! Your righteousness! And for Your forgiveness and love!

And thank You again for saving me and for giving me the words, the thoughts, the time, and the courage to write this book about You for my family, friends, and whomever else that would read this.

Father, glorify Yourself in all that You have created and done, and as Jesus asks, we wait for the day to see Your glory—face-to-face!

> The glory that you have given me I have given to them, that they may be one even as we are one, I in them and you in me, that they may become perfectly one, so that the world may know that you sent me and loved them even as you loved me. Father, I desire that they also, whom you have given me, may be with me where I am, to see my glory that you have given me because you loved me before the foundation of the world. O righteous Father, even though the world does not know you, I know you, and these know that you have sent me. I made known to them your name, and I will continue to make it known, that the love with which you have loved me may be in them, and I in them. (John 17:22–26)

In Jesus's name, Amen!

Parking Lot

Strive to always be in communion with God, to have a God consciousness.

Considering adding to the "'Building Is on Fire' Analogy" in chapter 3

Lazarus, Wake Up!

> Jesus said, "Take away the stone." Martha, the sister of the dead man, said to him, "Lord, by this time there will be an odor, for he has been dead four days." Jesus said to her, "Did I not tell you that if you believed you would see the glory of God?" So they took away the stone. And Jesus lifted up his eyes and said, "Father, I thank you that you have heard me. I knew that you always hear me, but I said this on account of the people standing around, that they may believe that you sent me." When he had said these things, he cried out with a loud voice, "Lazarus, come out." The man who had died came out, his hands and feet bound with linen strips, and his face wrapped with a cloth. Jesus said to them, "Unbind him, and let him go." (John 11:39–44)

Notice that Jesus has the power even over death, so why not also salvation? Lazarus was dead for four days. I submit that Jesus purposely waited until Lazarus's body was in the progressive state of decay.

What was Lazarus's response to the awakening by Jesus? He obeyed the voice of God—Jesus—and he came out of his tomb and was alive! When the Spirit calls someone, it is like Lazarus—they are made spiritually alive!

Union with Christ

> "I am the true vine, and my Father is the vine-dresser. Every branch in me that does not bear fruit he takes away, and every branch that does bear fruit he prunes, that it may bear more fruit. Already you are clean because of the word that I have spoken to you. Abide in me, and I in you. As the branch cannot bear fruit by itself, unless it abides in the vine, neither can you, unless you abide in me. I am the vine; you are the branches. Whoever abides in me and I in him, he it is that bears much fruit, for apart from me you can do nothing. (John 15:1–5)

Jesus is the vine.

Believers are His branches, and the Father is the vinedresser.

We have a grapevine within our backyard, and despite my lack of properly tending to it, it thrives. It is over 125 years old—being transplanted from my uncle's farm—and we even have moved it three times in our housing history, and it still abundantly produces grapes.

What I want to call out is that a grapevine starts from one center vine or trunk coming out from the ground and from there branches proceed out from the trunk. The trunk's purpose is to feed the branches, the water, and nutrients for the branches to produce grapes. Without the trunk and its purpose, the branches wither and break off and die.

Thus, to get grapes, the branches are 100 percent dependent upon the center vine, the trunk, and thus it is the trunk that sends to the branches everything the fruit needs to be.

So in God's sovereignty, Jesus declares we are His branches, and He works in us and though us to produce fruit. In effect, we are the conduit to do the good works of Christ that God has prepared for us to walk in.

> As the Father has loved me, so have I loved you. Abide in my love. If you keep my command-ments, you will abide in my love, just as I have kept my Father's commandments and abide in his love. These things I have spoken to you, that my joy may be in you, and that your joy may be full. (John 15:9–11)

> You did not choose me, but I chose you and appointed you that you should go and bear fruit and that your fruit should abide, so that whatever you ask the Father in my name, he may give it to you. (John 15:16)

The works of the vinedresser.

Jesus tells us that there are two qualifying descriptors of branches: non-alive—dead—no fruit, and those who are alive and bearing fruit and thus are pruned by the Father for more increase.

Is Jesus teaching that you can lose your salvation?

No.

Evidence to true believers and false believers?

Yes.

The branches that are broken off are the so-called disciples.

See John 6:37–39, John 10:26–30, and John 6:66.

Those that God cuts away—judgment.

Those that God prunes; cultivates, grows discipline (Heb. 12:6).

Jesus then tells the disciples that they are already clean, so is there a parallel between being alive in Christ and clean and being dead or unfruitful and taken away?

Now here is an interesting twist, or it is to me. Jesus tells His disciple to abide in Him. And then it gets further interesting—whoever abides in Christ (you and me) and Jesus in him.

The willingness to be pruned makes you clean already (see feet washing).

In John 5:24, past from death to life—already, everything is behind you.

A humble and contrite heart is an earmark to producing fruit.

Scriptural Index

Scripture referenced by books of the Bible

GENESIS
Genesis 20:1–7
Genesis 50:20–21
EXODUS
Exodus 4:21
Exodus 7:1–5
Exodus 14:1–4
NUMBERS
Numbers 22:20–35
DEUTERONOMY
Deuteronomy 7:6–8
Deuteronomy 9:4–6
Deuteronomy 29:2–4
Deuteronomy 30:6 (4x)
JOSHUA
Joshua 24:15
JUDGES
Judges 9:22–24
2 SAMUEL
2 Samuel 24:10
1 CHRONICLES
1 Chronicles 21:1
1 Chronicles 28:9–10

2 CHRONICLES
2 Chronicles 36:22–23
EZRA
Ezra 1:1–4
Ezra 1:5
JOB
Job 1:21–22
Job 2:10
Job 33:4
PSALMS
Psalms 19:1
Psalms 19:14
Psalms 23:2, 3
Psalms 29:1–11
Psalms 31:3
Psalms 51:1–12
Psalms 56:3–4
Psalms 74:17
Psalms 96:1–13
Psalms 97:1–12
Psalms 105:4
Psalms 115:3 (2x)
Psalms 139:12
Psalms 139:13–16

Mark 11:1–7
Mark 12:30–31
Mark 13:9–13
Mark 14:24
LUKE
Luke 1:15
Luke 1:26–33, 37–38
Luke 2:49–52
Luke 5:4–8
Luke 6:45
Luke 10:20–24
Luke 12:8
Luke 13:1–5
Luke 13:34–35
Luke 18:1
Luke 21:12–19
Luke 22: 3
Luke 22:19–20 (3x)
Luke 23:34
Luke 24:27
Luke 24:44–45 (2x)
JOHN
John 1:1–3 (2x)
John 1:12–13 (2x)
John 1:46–50
John 1:48
John 1:49
John 3:3
John 3:7
John 3:8
John 3:3–8
John 3:20–21
John 4:23
John 6:28–29
John 6:29
John 6:37–39

John 6:45 (3x)
John 6:63
John 6:60–65
John 6:60–71
John 13:23–26
John 8:31–32
John 8:34
John 9:1–7
John 10:16
John 12:27–30
John 15:26, 27
John 16:29–33
John 16:33
John 17:8–19
John 17:20–26 (2x)
John 17:24
John 19:1–11
John 20:27–29
John 21:15–19
John 21:20–22
ACTS
Acts 1:6–7
Acts 1:6–11
Acts 2:16–18 (2x)
Acts 2:22–24 (2x)
Acts 2:39
Acts 2:23
Acts 2:42–47
Acts 6:5 (2x)
Acts 9:15–17 (2x)
Acts 9:31
Acts 12:5
Acts 13:46–52
Acts 13:48
Acts 15:22–25
Acts 16:11–40

Acts 16:14
Acts 16:14–15
Acts 18:9–10
ROMANS
Romans 1:8–15
Romans 1:18–21
Romans 1:18–25 (2x)
Romans 3:10–12 (2x)
Romans 3:23
Romans 5:1–8
Romans 5:5 (2x)
Romans 5:12
Romans 6:17–19
Romans 8:2–11
Romans 8:6–8
Romans 8:14–19
Romans 8:16–17
Romans 8:18–21
Romans 8:26–28
Romans 8:28
Romans 8:28–30 (4x)
Romans 9:6–8 (2x)
Romans 9:10–24
Romans 9:6–8
Romans 9:14–24
Romans 9:15–16
Romans 10:9–13
Romans 10:1–4
Romans 10:18–11:10
Romans 11:8–10
Romans 11:11–12
Romans 12:2
Romans 12:3
Romans 13:14
Romans 14:10–12
Romans 14:23

Romans 16:25–27
Romans 16:27
1 Corinthians
1 Corinthians 1:7–9
1 Corinthians 1:10–17
1 Corinthians 1:21–24
1 Corinthians 1:26–31 (2x)
1 Corinthians 2:3–16 (2x)
1 Corinthians 2:10–17
1 Corinthians 3:5–7
1 Corinthians 4:19
1 Corinthians 5:1–13
1 Corinthians 6:9–11
1 Corinthians 7:17–24
1 Corinthians 10:31
1 Corinthians 11:17–34
1 Corinthians 11:25 (2x)
1 Corinthians 10:31
1 Corinthians 12:1–31
1 Corinthians 12:3
1 Corinthians 12:12–13
1 Corinthians 12:18
1 Corinthians 12:27–31
1 Corinthians 13:1–3
1 Corinthians 13:31
1 Corinthians 14:1–5
1 Corinthians 15:1–2
1 Corinthians 15:10 (3x)
1 Corinthians 15:54–58
2 CORINTHIANS
2 Corinthians 2:7
2 Corinthians 3:1–6 (2x)
2 Corinthians 4:4–6
2 Corinthians 4:4
2 Corinthians 4:4–6
2 Corinthians 4:3–6

2 Corinthians 4:4
2 Corinthians 4:4–6
2 Corinthians 5:7
2 Corinthians 7:10
2 Corinthians 13:5 (2x)
GALATIANS
Galatians 1:1–3
Galatians 1:11–17
Galatians 1:15–17 (2x)
Galatians 3:1–9
Galatians 3:22
Galatians 4:6
Galatians 4:6–7
Galatians 5:16
Galatians 5:16–26 (3x)
EPHESIANS
Ephesians 1:1
Ephesians 1:3–14
Ephesians 1:4–6
Ephesians 1:4–11
Ephesians 1:11–12
Ephesians 1:15–21
Ephesians 1:17–19 (4x)
Ephesians 2:1–3
Ephesians 2:1–10 (2x)
Ephesians 2:8
Ephesians 2:8–10 (3x)
Ephesians 2:10 (3x)
Ephesians 2:22
Ephesians 3:14–21
Ephesians 4:1–7
Ephesians 4:13 (2x)
Ephesians 4:22–24
Ephesians 4:29–32
Ephesians 5:18
Ephesians 5:15–21

Ephesians 6:18–20
Ephesians 6:19–20
PHILIPPIANS
Philippians 1:6 (2x)
Philippians 1:3–11
Philippians 2:13 (2x)
Philippians 2:10–11
Philippians 2:12–13 (2x)
Philippians 2:9–11
Philippians 3:3
Philippians 3:4–8
Philippians 3:12
Philippians 3:12–17
Philippians 4:4–9
Philippians 4:11–13 (2x)
COLOSSIANS
Colossians 1:15–20 (2x)
Colossians 1:15–23 (2x)
Colossians 1:21–23
Colossians 1:9–10
Colossians 1:9–14
Colossians 2:13
Colossians 3:1–4
Colossians 3:9–10
Colossians 1:10–12
1 THESSALONIANS
1 Thessalonians 1:10
1 Thessalonians 2:12
1 Thessalonians 2:12–13
1 Thessalonians 5:9–11
1 Thessalonians 5:16–22
1 Thessalonians 5:17–18
1 Thessalonians 5:23–24
2 THESSALONIANS
2 Thessalonians 1:5–12
2 Thessalonians 2:1–3

2 Thessalonians 2:1–14
2 Thessalonians 2:11 (2x)
2 Thessalonians 2:13 (2x)
1 TIMOTHY
1 Timothy 1:17
1 Timothy 2:4
1 Timothy 2:3–7 (3x)
1 Timothy 2:6
1 Timothy 4:13–16
2 TIMOTHY
2 Timothy 1:3–7
2 Timothy 1:6
2 Timothy 1:8–10
2 Timothy 2:8–13
2 Timothy 2:24–26 (2x)
2 Timothy 3:12–13
2 Timothy 4:1
2 Timothy 4:3–5
TITUS
Titus 1:7–12
Titus 2:1–14
PHILEMON
Philemon 1:6
HEBREWS
Hebrews 8:6–10 (2x)
Hebrews 10:23–25
Hebrews 11: 1–3
Hebrews 9:15 (3x)
Hebrews 13:20–21 (2x)
JAMES
James 1:2–4 (2x)
James 1:5
James 1:12
James 1:17–18
James 1:19–21
James 4:13–15

1 PETER
1 Peter 1:1–2 (2x)
1 Peter 1:3–5 (2x)
1 Peter 1:10–12
1 Peter 2:9–10 (2x)
1 Peter 4:12–19
1 Peter 5:6–11 (2x)
1 Peter 5:10
2 PETER
2 Peter 1:1
2 Peter 1:5–7, 10
2 Peter 1:16–17
2 Peter 3:8–9
2 Peter 3:9
2 Peter 3:18
1 JOHN
1 John 5:1
1 John 3:14–15
1 John 3:21–24
1 John 4:19
1 John 5:1
1 John 5:4 (2x)
1 John 5:5
1 John 5:6–12, 20 (2x)
1 John 5:18 (2x)
1 John 5:20 (2x)
JUDE
Jude 1:24–25 (3x)
REVELATION
Revelation 2:10–11
Revelation 4:2–11
Revelation 4:11 (3x)
Revelation 13:8
Revelation 16:9
Revelation 17:17
Revelation 22:17

Subject Index

About the Author

David recently retired from the corporate IT sales world that spanned a thirty-two-year career and was blessed by God in all the roles he held during this time. Also, David spent time in his early work years as a machinist in the steel industry and as a trained musician from Carnegie Mellon University.

Today, as with David's vocations of his past, God is now leading him—this time to write. Although not a pastor, nor formally trained at a Bible college, David is a disciple of Jesus, approaching fifty years of faith. A faith not of his own merit, he would say, but one of Christ's holding him each day. So within these pages are of David's love of Jesus, of his notes in study through the years. From his notes of teaching adult Sunday school lessons to sharing the gospel at work, neighborhood, or the grocery store. And of his passion for the Gospel to reach all who will believe!

He is married to a wonderful wife, Sandy, of thirty-nine years, and blessed with two adult children and four grandchildren. When not writing, he enjoys going to car cruises and hearing all the stories that people tell about their cars, for life's journey involves people and not the cars, per se, although he has a car of his own.

CPSIA information can be obtained
at www.ICGtesting.com
Printed in the USA
LVHW031744130821
695221LV00005BB/269